Jesus Was Human Too

Jesus Was Human Too

SEEING THE SON OF GOD IN LIFE'S EVERYDAY MOMENTS

RYAN LOKKESMOE

Our Daily Bread Publishing®

Jesus Was Human Too: Seeing the Son of God in Life's Everyday Moments

Published in association with Books & Such Literary Management, www.booksandsuch.com.

Interior design by Michael J. Williams

ISBN: 978-1-64070-441-1

Library of Congress Cataloging-in-Publication Data Available

Printed in the United States of America
26 27 28 29 30 31 32 33 / 8 7 6 5 4 3 2 1

For my kids, Luke and Nora,
and my nieces and nephews:
Caroline, Wesley, Jackson, Jameson, and Madison

Jesus called the children to him and said, "Let the little children come to me, and do not hinder them, for the kingdom of God belongs to such as these."

Luke 18:16

Contents

INTRODUCTION

More Than Biology

Do you believe in Jesus?

If so, what you probably mean is that you believe in his divinity: his eternality, his miracles, his resurrection, his sovereignty over history and the universe, and the rest of his awe-inspiring attributes.

But do you also believe in Jesus's *humanity*?

You might respond to my question with something like, "Of course I believe in Jesus's humanity. He's fully human and fully divine. That's basic, historic Christian theology." You might also wonder what belief has to do with Jesus's humanity. His human life is a well-established historical fact, and facts don't require faith.

True, but that's not where I was going with my question. Let me ask it another way: Do you *trust* in Jesus's humanity?

You might answer, "What's there to trust? It happened, and I believe it. He lived life here on earth. He taught, he confronted the Pharisees, he turned over the tables, he felt pain on the cross."

Granted, but those are the extraordinary parts of his human

life that related to his unique rescue mission, the kinds of things that you and I can't replicate in our own experiences.

So, let me ask again: Do you believe in Jesus's humanity? Not in the extraordinary ways that he was human, but in the ordinary, daily ways? Have you spent any time imagining it?

Can you envision Jesus getting angry for being underpaid? Can you picture him taking a walk by himself, sniffling and kicking the dirt after hearing that a family member was ominously sick? Can you hear the clanking of his tools, tossed into the corner after a long day's work? Can you imagine him collapsing with an exhausted sigh on his bed? Can you hear the laughter of his younger siblings playing in the street, or his mother's voice calling out a reminder to pick up something at the market? Can you see Jesus's clenched jaw as he pays an unjust tax to the local authorities?

I'd like to think I have believed in Jesus's humanity throughout my journey of faith, but I've recently concluded that I've passively doubted some of it, or at least thought superficially about it. Perhaps you have too.

Secular people doubt Jesus's divinity, but we Christians seem to have the opposite struggle: we doubt his humanity. We struggle to believe his human experiences have any bearing on our lives today. We think the purpose of Jesus's years on earth was mainly to pass time until he was old enough to be crucified.

One of the challenges is that Jesus's humanity is often spoken of as a theological abstraction, with precise but esoteric terms like *incarnation*. When discussing the nature of Christ, as the early Christians did in their writings and councils, we affirm that Jesus was simultaneously fully human and fully divine. But speaking of Jesus's humanity in theological terms can make his human nature seem unreal or unrelatable.

Also, we are not adept at balancing Jesus's divinity and

humanity in our minds, because they seem contradictory. This puts us at risk of subtly adopting unbiblical perspectives. Ancient Christians fought against a heresy called Docetism, which claimed that Jesus wasn't really human—he just appeared to be human. We must guard against believing that Jesus was fully God but only *mostly* human.

To counter our tendency to think of Jesus's humanity as theoretical, we must deliberately reflect on his ordinary human experiences: his real, ground-level, laundry-doing, ear-infection-having, insomnia-coping, annoyance-feeling humanity.

But we must also be careful not to limit our reflections to mere biology. We may focus on Jesus getting tired, being hungry, sweating, bleeding, and so on. This is all true, but we humans are much more than our physiology. We cannot relegate his humanity to a collection of organs, tissues, bones, and hormones; animals have those too. His biology *and* his experiences made him like us.

But even if we do accept that Jesus was truly human in experiential ways, there is another hazard to avoid: believing that his life was not that hard for him. Jesus is God in the flesh, so he couldn't have *really* struggled as we do, right? He must have been insulated from the normal challenges of life, as if he rolled around Galilee in a celestial hamster ball that shielded him from the problems and pains we face.

But that is not true. Jesus's life—though extraordinary—was also quite ordinary. Remember that when Jesus began his public ministry, people who knew him responded with questions like:

> Isn't this Joseph's son? (Luke 4:22)
>
> Isn't this the carpenter's son? Isn't his mother's name Mary, and aren't his brothers James, Joseph, Simon and Judas? Aren't all his sisters with us? (Matthew 13:55–56)

> Is this not Jesus, the son of Joseph, whose father and mother we know? How can he now say, "I came down from heaven"? (John 6:42)

These questions reveal how ordinary Jesus seemed to people who knew him up to that point. Jesus was indeed more than a carpenter,[1] but he was also merely a carpenter.

In Hebrews 4, the author explains that Jesus is our great high priest and describes him with these stirring words: "For we do not have a high priest who is unable to empathize with our weaknesses, but we have one who has been tempted in every way, just as we are—yet he did not sin" (v. 15). To grasp the richness of these phrases, we must consider what is meant (and not meant) by "tempted." Because the verse ends with that comment about Jesus not sinning, it's natural to interpret "tempted" as referring mainly to sinful temptations. But that is not exactly what is in view here. The New Testament was originally written in ancient Greek, and the Greek word rendered into our English Bibles as "tempted" is *peirazō*, which refers to something being "tested." This can signify temptation to sin but also includes many other experiences that put one to the test.[2]

In the ancient Greek translation of the Old Testament, this term *peirazō* was chosen to describe Abraham being tested by God through the command to sacrifice Isaac. It also appears in the narrative when the queen of Sheba visited Solomon to test his wisdom and when Daniel invited his Babylonian overlords to test him and his friends by allowing them to eat only vegetables for ten days. These are all examples of testing that do not refer to avoiding sin.

So, we should not understand the statement in Hebrews that Jesus "has been tempted in every way" to mean simply that he was enticed by a wide variety of potential sins, though he undoubtedly was. It means that Jesus was *tested* in all the ways that we are: physically, emotionally, spiritually, relationally. Jesus explored the deep inner caverns and wild outer landscapes of human experience.

Here's the point: our humanity is not something theoretical to God; he personally experienced what it's like to be us.

If we believe Jesus was tested in every way like we are, then we must conclude that he had all the ordinary experiences that we do. He had fond memories and disappointing ones. He had favorite foods. He looked forward to things. He told jokes. He brooded. He got along with some people better than others. He had a most embarrassing story. He rolled his eyes. He felt attraction. He had conversations he wished had gone differently. He struggled to provide. He laughed so hard that water (or maybe wine) came out of his nose. Perhaps he fake laughed when he felt it was polite. He felt the big feelings of adolescence. He had neighbors and coworkers who frustrated him. He played and argued with his siblings. Things happened that Jesus wished he could forget.

You are human, and so am I. Jesus was human too, and he stands ready to encourage us from a position of genuine understanding.[3] We can place our trust in his humanity as we do in his divinity. He knows what our lives are like. When he observes our days, hears our prayers, and peers into our hearts, a lifetime of his own ordinary human experiences enables him to genuinely empathize. This is a profoundly reassuring thought.

But what if we lack faith in Jesus's humanity or maintain a shallow awareness of it? One consequence is that we will find it hard to believe the depth of God's love for us. Honest Christians will admit that we sometimes struggle to believe God loves us unconditionally. It seems too good to be true. One of the root causes for this disbelief is that we don't really believe he knows what it's like to be us. He can't relate. He doesn't get it. A God who does not understand us can seem remote, mysterious, and perhaps uncaring.

Trusting in Jesus's humanity is one remedy for this tendency to doubt God's love. It's a way to see God no longer as remote but close. No longer uncaring but deeply sympathetic. No longer mysterious but familiar.

When you've been through something painful or unsettling, meeting someone who has experienced the same thing can be comforting. You're not alone. You're understood. Someone has walked this path before you or is currently on the road with you. When you believe someone understands your situation, you let down your guard. You open your heart and mind to them in new ways.

Do you think of Jesus in this way? As someone who understands you because he has been there? He does understand, and we can discover life-giving comfort in that.

In each of the chapters that follow, we will explore a facet of Jesus's humanity. We will search the Scriptures and history to gain a better sense of his relational life, financial life, political life, emotional life, and so on. With a clearer view of his experiences, we will consider our own lives and how Jesus navigated similar terrain.

Before we begin, a couple orienting comments are in order. First, while this book is focused on Jesus's human experiences during his time on earth, I want to state clearly at the outset that I simultaneously affirm Christ's divinity. My emphasis on his ordinary humanity should not be construed as coming at the expense of his divinity—his extraordinariness. But I will not continue to reiterate this point throughout the book, so please bear this in mind as we keep our focus on Jesus's human experiences during his years among us.

Second, all modern works that deal with ancient history include some degree of conjecture because the sources are fragmentary. However, I will make every effort to offer only plausible speculations, informed by the biblical text and other historical sources. You might think of this book as an impressionist painting of Jesus's human experiences. While an impressionist painter might give an accurate sense of landscape and light, we do not expect photorealism from the artist. In that spirit, I will strive to make enough historical brushstrokes that the resulting work is an accurate impression of Jesus's ordinary human life.

It is no small endeavor to write about Jesus. I confess I have felt a little uneasy about inadvertently misrepresenting him in some way. When I shared this anxiety with my wife, Ashley, she reminded me of the marvelous truth that I can ask Jesus—the subject of this book—to help me represent him well. So, that's what I have done. I have prayed that the Lord would guide my words in such a way that Christ would be glorified and that you, the reader, would experience new depths of joy in your relationship with him.

By the end of this book, I hope to convince you that we modern Christians have been mostly agnostic about Jesus's humanity, and that if we'll open our hearts to a fuller picture of our savior, we will discover new hues of hope and deeper channels of comfort. To you, my brothers and sisters in Christ, I ask this question: How might your relationship with God deepen and sweeten if you leave behind the flattened facade of how you've been picturing Jesus's humanity, and begin to trust fully in his actual humanness?

Allow me to close this introduction by speaking to an audience I hope is reading this book alongside us Christians: those who are skeptical of the claims of Christianity. If that's you, whether you're an atheist, agnostic, or something else, I'm glad you're reading this. Maybe a Christian friend or family member gave you this book as a gift. If so, I hope you'll converse with them and share some of your candid reflections. It's my hope that you find these pages to be encouraging and thought-provoking. I ask you this question: If God exists, and that God chose to live as Jesus did, what would you think of him? Perhaps you'll meet God not in the miracles and the extraordinary but in the ordinary life he chose to live—one not so different from your own.

QUESTIONS FOR GROUP DISCUSSION OR PERSONAL REFLECTION

- How often do you think of Jesus's human experiences? When you do, what comes to mind?
- How do you think your faith might deepen by reflecting on Jesus's ordinary life?
- In what ways do you hope to grow by reading this book?

Dear Jesus, please help me grow closer to you by reading this book. I confess that it is difficult to imagine you experiencing anything like I do, but I believe that you did. As I read the following pages, please magnify my imagination and help me to see you more clearly. Help me to deepen my understanding of how well you know me and how much you love me. I trust that you will. Amen.

1

A Mixed-Up Home Life

My birthday is in the middle of January, and every year I sense a plainness around that time, a palpable void of energy in the community. The reason, of course, is that my birthday falls a couple weeks after Christmas and New Year's Eve—summits of yearly festivity. In those early days of each new year, twinkling lights retreat from rooflines, sleigh bells exit our music, and bare Christmas trees lie curbside. Everything seems a little bit muted.

We're going to begin our exploration of Jesus's humanness by looking at his family life during the earliest years of his time on earth. To do that, we need to look at his early childhood with a plain, mid-January perspective, removed from the glow of the holiday season. Put another way, we have to de-Christmas Jesus's life so we can see him with fresh eyes and discover the ordinary and relatable elements of his family's experience. So, we won't focus on angelic apparitions, nativity scenes, or miraculous lights in the sky. In our non-holiday investigation, we will unearth a set of family experiences that were challenging, disorienting, at times painful, and ever-changing. We will start before Jesus's birth, and then track his family's movements during his childhood.

NAZARETH

We meet Mary and Joseph in the opening pages of the gospels of Matthew and Luke, where we are told that the two residents of Nazareth are pledged to be married (Matthew 1:18; Luke 1:27; 2:4–5). This is the language of betrothal or engagement.[1] Ancient engagements were more serious and final than our modern notions of becoming engaged. When the angel Gabriel told Mary that she would be the one to bear the Son of God, she was already in a legally binding marriage contract with Joseph, but the wedding itself was still in the future.[2]

Mary also learned from Gabriel that her relative Elizabeth had miraculously conceived in her old age. Luke tells us that Mary then hurried to a town in Judea to visit Elizabeth (Luke 1:36–40). We are not told why she took this trip, but it seems to have happened rather quickly. It could be that Mary wanted to confirm Gabriel's words by investigating whether Elizabeth was, in fact, pregnant. It could be that she just wanted moral support in the early days of her pregnancy, possibly as she worked up the courage to share the news with Joseph. Maybe both. Luke tells us that Mary spent about three months away and then returned north to Nazareth (v. 56). It's possible Mary was showing signs of being pregnant by that time or would be very soon.

If it were known in Nazareth that Mary was pregnant before her wedding to Joseph, that would not necessarily have been viewed as scandalous, as long as people believed that Joseph was the baby's father. Premarital sex was not much of a concern in this situation; the two were already in a binding marriage contract. The potential scandal would have been a private one: Joseph knowing that someone else was the father and believing that Mary had been unfaithful.[3] In what probably felt to Joseph like a sad and confusing time (before he understood what was really going on), he made plans to discreetly separate from Mary (Matthew 1:19). Joseph was well within social norms and his legal rights to seek a divorce, but he did not wish to go about this painful and embarrassing separation in a way that would shame Mary. But God gave Joseph the clarity he needed, and the couple carried on, anticipating God's impending miracle.

BETHLEHEM

In the middle of intertwining their lives and coming to grips with God's intentions for the child growing in Mary's womb, the couple had to contend with a government mandate. The imperial census required everyone to travel to their own town (Luke 2:3). This tells us that, legally, Bethlehem was considered Joseph's hometown. At minimum, it means Joseph owned land in Bethlehem, because the Romans kept records of their subjects based on where they owned taxable fields.[4] It is also possible that Joseph lived in Bethlehem at least part of the time. The journey from Nazareth in the north to Bethlehem in the south would have taken several days.

The common view that Mary and Joseph arrived in Bethlehem and found that there was no vacancy at the inn is not exactly what happened. Close readers of Luke's grammar have noticed this for centuries.[5] The Greek word in Luke 2:7 traditionally translated as "inn" does not refer specifically to a hotel but more generically to some sort of lodging—perhaps a guest room.[6] The Greek word is *katalyma*, which is the same word used when Jesus instructs his disciples to locate a room in which they can celebrate the Passover together (Mark 14:14; Luke 22:11). When Luke related the parable of the good Samaritan, which features an actual inn, he used a different Greek word, *pandocheion*, that refers specifically to what we think of as a hotel (Luke 10:34). If Luke intended for us to think of Mary and Joseph looking for a hotel room in Bethlehem, he probably would have used this same unmistakable word.

Because Bethlehem was Joseph's hometown, he or his family probably had a house there—the natural place for him and Mary to stay for a while. The couple would not need to find an inn. It was during this time in Bethlehem, before Jesus was born, that the wedding probably happened. Marriage was a two-step process that started with betrothal and ended with the wedding itself, which was when the bride first began to live with her husband.[7] When Mary and Joseph were on their journey from Nazareth, they were still engaged. Luke makes that clear: Joseph went to Bethlehem "to register with Mary, who was pledged to be married to him and was expecting a child" (2:5).

Mary and Joseph appear to have been in Bethlehem for some time before Jesus's birth, indicated by Luke's language: "*While they were there*, the time came for the baby to be born" (v. 6, emphasis added). Probably they had been staying in a guest room at Joseph's family home when Mary went into labor.[8] But, it may not have been a suitable venue for Jesus's birth. The challenge was not a hotel with no vacancy but rather a guest room with not enough space for Mary to give birth.[9] First-century homes had a main room where the family and visitors would congregate, which would be the preferable (and typical) location for a childbirth, providing ample space for female relatives to assist. These larger rooms usually housed animals as well, so it would not have been unusual for a manger to be present.[10]

So, when we picture Mary and Joseph's arrival in Bethlehem, we should not imagine them scrambling through an unfamiliar town, frantically searching for a hotel with vacancy, failing to do so, and Mary giving birth to Jesus almost immediately in a strange barn. What makes more sense—both biblically and historically—is that Mary and Joseph arrived in town and connected with Joseph's family. Wedding plans were made, and the pair was married. Sometime later, Jesus made his appearance.[11]

Most of us have stories to tell about our parents' lives before we were born and about the day we arrived on the scene. At the time of my birth, my parents lived in California. My mom was an event coordinator at a country club, and my dad was a sheriff's deputy. After my mom went into labor, my parents were stuck in a terrible traffic jam on the way to the hospital. A year later, halfway across the country, my future father-in-law hailed a taxi in Tulsa, Oklahoma—something he never did—to make it to the hospital in time for the birth of his daughter Ashley, who became my wife twenty-three years later.

My son had long, feathery blond hair when he was born. All the nurses talked about it. My mother-in-law stayed with us for a week or so after we left the hospital and helped us with many things. My daughter was born two years later with this adorable little heart-shaped face. Her big brother was eager to meet her but mostly interested in the various light switches in the hospital room. Both of my children were born in Houston but at different hospitals. Friends came to visit, and family drove in from out of town for both occasions.

Jesus had stories like this too. His parents were real people like you and me. They were not props in a nativity scene. They were engaged and married like most people their age. Joseph had a job. They had parents, friends, and neighbors whose opinions they cared about. They coped with the simultaneously joyful and unsettling announcement about their child's future and had to leave town for reasons outside of their control. They had family who celebrated Jesus's birth with them and probably helped the new parents in the unforgettable first months of Jesus's life. Years later, they would have beamed when telling young Jesus about the day he was born, and like most kids I've ever met, his eyes would have lit up during the story.

Unlike most of us, on the other hand, Mary and Joseph had to deal with the disruptions and uncertainty of living under the thumb of an autocrat. More than one autocrat, in fact. Caesar forced their relocation from Nazareth to Bethlehem. It was Herod who forced them to move even farther away.

EGYPT

There is a sense of immediacy when we read the gospel accounts of Jesus's youngest years. This is partly because the Scriptures do not describe everything that happened. The timeline is compressed to give us the highlights. For example, the Magi probably did not visit Jesus on the day of his birth but arrived sometime later. After coming to Jerusalem and conversing with Herod, they found Jesus at a house in Bethlehem—perhaps Joseph's family home where Mary had given birth (Matthew 2:11). When the Magi left and returned to their country, Herod was infuriated and sought to kill all the boys in Bethlehem under the age of two (v. 16). This grim age range was based on the timeline outlined by the Magi. Herod was under the impression, after his conversation with the Magi, that Jesus may have been born up to two years prior. Joseph was warned in a dream to flee with his family, so he left with Mary and Jesus—who was either an infant or a toddler—and headed southwest toward Egypt.

To our minds, Egypt seems like a foreign environment compared to Nazareth or Bethlehem, in part because of Egypt's interactions with Israel many centuries earlier in the Old Testament. In a sense that's true: Egypt was quite different. But by the time of Jesus, Egypt had been under the rule of the Greeks and Romans for centuries. So, there was a lot in common culturally between Roman-ruled Egypt and Roman-ruled Judea. Also, Jews had been moving out of their historic homeland for centuries and had established large and flourishing communities around the Mediterranean world.[12] In Egypt alone, some ancient estimates put the Jewish population at more than a million, though this is probably a somewhat exaggerated figure.[13] So, while Egypt was indeed a far-off and unfamiliar place for Jesus's family to move, there were long-established groups of Jews in that area. Mary and Joseph would not have had to look hard to find Jewish communities where they could live, work, and worship.

The years in Egypt were formative ones in Jesus's life, when he learned to run, talk, play with friends, and maybe even write. His earliest memories of synagogue services probably came from this time. Jesus may have also become a big brother in Egypt. Mary and Joseph undoubtedly would have invested in friendships, especially because their families were living far away. It is very possible they had relatives already living in Egypt, but we don't know that for sure. I imagine that in the years to come, Mary and Joseph would have kept in touch with friends from their years in Egypt, perhaps reuniting occasionally at festivals in Jerusalem.

I've lived in several states: California, New York, Texas, Massachusetts, Colorado, and South Carolina. On some of those moves, when I was a kid, I was carried along. My brother, Sean, and I had no say; we just had to adjust to new cities, cultures, and schools. I still remember how strange it was to hear the word *y'all* for the first time when moving to Texas as an elementary schooler. It was sad and disorienting to move as a child but also exciting and full of new opportunities. Other moves, after growing up, were by choice. I've enjoyed living in some places more than in others. I was able to make lasting friendships more easily in some places than in others. I have unevenly kept up with friends and acquaintances from these various locations that represent different phases of my life. Jesus and his family must have experienced an ancient version of this.

BACK TO NAZARETH

It's not clear how long Jesus's family lived in Egypt. It seems to have been a few years based on Matthew's description (2:19–23). Taken together with their time in Bethlehem, they may have been away from Nazareth for three to five years, or a little longer. When they eventually returned to Nazareth, Mary and Joseph's friends, family, and neighbors would have been excited and maybe a little surprised to meet their budding family. Compared to Egypt, which had large, multilingual urban centers and a vast population spread across the countryside, Nazareth was provincial and somewhat remote.[14] At the time, there were perhaps two hundred people living in the town.[15]

I remember moving to Massachusetts for seminary after growing up in Texas, and how some people there could detect my mild Southern accent. Of course, when I used the word *y'all*, they noticed it every time (just like I noticed every misplaced *R* in their New England accent). It's possible that Jesus spoke his childlike Aramaic with a not-so-Galilean accent, and that his family used some words or expressions they acquired in Egypt that seemed unusual to their neighbors in Nazareth.[16] Jesus may also have picked up some Greek in Egypt, where it was spoken more commonly than in Galilee.

A GROWING FAMILY

In the little-described years that followed, we know that Jesus's family grew substantially. He became a big brother many times over. This means, of course, that his mom was pregnant much of the time he was growing up. Jesus would have started to learn the family trade from Joseph as he approached adolescence, and as the eldest son he had increasing family responsibilities.

In Matthew's gospel, some of Jesus's siblings are named: James, Joseph, Simon, and Judas. Locals who knew Jesus's family spoke of "all his sisters" (13:55–56). So, Jesus had four brothers and at least two sisters, though the phrasing "all his sisters" implies more than two. It seems Jesus had at least six or seven younger siblings. Including himself, Mary, and Joseph, his immediate family may have been as large as ten people, and if his family was like most during that era, there were cousins, aunts, uncles, and grandparents living nearby.

We have no description of Jesus's relationship with his siblings during their growing-up years, but we know that by the time he began his public ministry, some or all of Jesus's brothers and sisters did not believe in him. In John's gospel, we learn that his brothers taunted him about proving his identity to the world: "Jesus' brothers said to him, 'Leave Galilee and go to Judea, so that your disciples there may see the works you do. No one who wants to become a public figure acts in secret. Since you are doing these things, show yourself to the world.' For even his own brothers did not believe in him" (7:3–5).

In the gospel of Mark, we learn that some of his family members tried to rein him in, asserting that he was deranged (3:21). We don't know why his siblings had difficulty supporting his mission. It could be that he had a strained relationship with some of them, extending back to their childhood. It could be that they had heard the miraculous story about Jesus's birth one too many times and resented the way their parents doted on him. It could be that they were embarrassed by Jesus and tried to explain it all to friends and neighbors as him having lost his mind. Maybe they were jealous. We don't know. All we know is that during the time when Jesus was winning over thousands of people, his siblings—on the whole—were unconvinced.[17] This may not mean they all rejected Jesus in forceful fashion. It could simply be that siblings have a knack for being unimpressed by each other. Whatever the case, we're on safe ground assuming it hurt Jesus's feelings.

OUR EVERYDAY MOMENTS

When we reflect on Jesus's early years with our non-holiday lenses, we see that his family moved several times to different regions for various reasons. They experienced the frustrating disorientation of moving, just like we feel untethered when we experience significant change. Maybe you have experienced cross-country moves or other major life changes that have turned your routines and expectations upside down. If you have, you can rest assured that Jesus has similar memories and really does know what it's like. If you've recently met someone who is new to your community, or perhaps to your church, maybe you can encourage them by pointing out that Jesus experienced something similar and offering to pray for them or help them get settled in some tangible way.

As he grew up, Jesus's family enlarged, and his sibling relationships, however healthy they might have been in his younger years, took a painful turn during his public ministry. If you have a strained relationship with a sibling, or any family member for that matter, then you know the pain, disappointment, and feelings of helplessness that often accompany that experience. If you are limping through a painful landscape like that, Jesus really does understand what it's like, and he hurts with you. When you pray for help and healing—whether for yourself or for someone else in your life—you can trust that Jesus remembers how it feels and truly empathizes.

So, we begin to see how mixed-up Jesus's life would have

felt, especially compared to his peers who tended to live in one place for most of their life. Our lives can feel mixed-up too, and Jesus understands. He had a good family, but his growing-up years were not rosy. They were relatable, though, and that's comforting.

QUESTIONS FOR GROUP DISCUSSION OR PERSONAL REFLECTION

- What surprised or challenged you about this chapter?
- What does it say about God that he chose a family life that wasn't always easy?
- How do you see your own life reflected in Jesus's family story?
- In what ways do you need to trust Jesus with your family life?
- What is one step you can take this week to have a healthier relationship with your family?
- If you could ask Jesus something about your family life and get an audible answer right now, what would you ask and why?

Dear Jesus, thank you for choosing to live life within a family. You didn't have to do that. You could have come to earth and lived alone, self-sufficient, apart from the joys and sorrows of family life. But you didn't. You chose to walk through life as we do. It's comforting to know you understand all the contours of my family life, the bright spots and dark corners. And you understand everything I have felt and am feeling now toward my family. Thank you for coming to save me, but thank you also for the way you came to save me, entering into my experiences so you can understand me and the rest of the world as much as possible. Help me to know just how much you love me. Amen.

2

A Strenuous Work Life

"So, what do you do?"

It's a familiar question. We hear it or say it when meeting new people, usually on the heels of the first lull in the conversation. It feels like an obvious, almost inevitable thing to say. The only uncertainty is who will ask first. In fact, we have such a shared expectation about this question that we don't even have to specify what we're asking about. Everyone who asks or answers the question knows that the topic is work.

In the West, and perhaps especially here in ever-industrious America, work is always at the front of our minds and on the tip of our tongues. Despite many other meaningful dimensions of our lives—family, faith, hobbies, and friendships—work is the topic that has a way of pushing itself to the front of the line. In a way, this is understandable. We spend many of our waking hours working, so it makes sense that we're interested in learning how other people spend their time and sharing with them how we spend ours.

But it's more than that. We look to our work for a deeper sense of worth and purpose. Again, this makes sense. It's not unhealthy to care about our work and pour ourselves into it. But sometimes we can go too far and empty too much of ourselves into it, expecting our jobs to provide soul-level meaning and identity. This can stray into exhausting and idolatrous territory, asking from our work what only God can give.

Jesus had a work life too. His perspective on work would have been somewhat different from ours, for a couple reasons. First, he lived in the ancient world where most people were poor and did manual labor for a living. There are similar communities in the modern world, and in these contexts work is rarely viewed as a source of identity or self-worth; it's just work. It's a means to staying secure and healthy. Second, Jesus did not sin. So, it's safe to say his view of his work did not stray into idolatry.

But Jesus did work, just like we do. There are seasons to our working lives, of course, and they are shaped by our stage of life and the opportunities available: full-time employee, part-time employee, job seeker, retiree, student, stay-at-home parent, volunteer, mentor, caregiver. Regardless of how we currently describe our work, we can all relate to certain elements of Jesus's work life. Let's consider what Jesus did for a living, how his job compared to other occupations at the time, and what we can learn from his work experiences.

JESUS'S JOB

In the Gospels, we learn that Jesus was a carpenter and that his father, Joseph, was too. When Jesus began his public ministry, locals asked a pair of questions about him: "Isn't this the carpenter's son?" and "Isn't this the carpenter?" (Matthew 13:55; Mark 6:3). These two questions are virtually interchangeable, because it was common for sons to follow in their father's footsteps and join the family trade. To ask if someone was a carpenter's son was nearly equivalent to asking if he was (or planned to become) a carpenter.[1] Jesus had probably been working as a carpenter in the vicinity of Nazareth for about two decades before he began his public ministry.[2]

But what do we mean by *carpenter*? Our modern English word *carpenter* means a woodworker, but the ancient Greek word used in the New Testament to describe Jesus's occupation had a broader sense. The word is *tektōn*, which meant something like a builder, craftsman, or artisan—someone who worked with wood but also with stone, metal, and other materials.[3] Because there was not much spare wood available where Jesus lived, the term *carpenter* is probably a little misleading when we think about Jesus's family trade.[4] *Builder* or *craftsman* gets closer to the heart of what Jesus did for a living.

At the time of Jesus's life, Nazareth was not a large town. There were probably a few hundred residents, so we might think of Jesus's family as local contractors doing a variety of projects for their friends and neighbors, and in nearby locales as opportunities presented themselves. They may have had a shop in Nazareth, or they may have worked at the site of their projects. Maybe both. This kind of work was feast or famine; sometimes they would have more work than they could keep up with. Sometimes they would have wished for more projects.

Many of us have had jobs with this kind of ebb and flow. After college, one of my jobs was teaching guitar lessons to children. This was one of a few part-time jobs I cobbled together in the lead-up to getting married and starting seminary. Sometimes I had more students than I could effectively handle. At other times, when the students' families were out of town or unavailable, I couldn't work as much. As a result, my pay fluctuated. Around the same time, my mom owned a clothing store in a historic downtown square. She experienced the same thing: feast or famine. At some times of the year, especially around the holidays, it was hard to keep up. At other times, she did whatever she could just to get people to walk through the door.

These kinds of jobs can be mentally and emotionally exhausting. When things aren't going well, you need to constantly hustle and drum up new business. There was an entrepreneurial element to Jesus's trade too. I can imagine him and his family members canvassing the vicinity, trying to find out if anyone needed their services. Even when things are going well, these jobs are taxing because the work comes in waves. Sometimes those waves are overwhelming and it's tough to keep up. And even if you can keep up, there's always the knowledge that the money won't remain as plentiful, so you need to save and plan for leaner seasons. Anyone who has ever owned their own business, set their own hours, or been their own boss understands how this feels.

JESUS'S SOCIOECONOMIC STATUS

But how did Jesus's work compare to other occupations at the time? Most people in the Roman world were poor by modern standards, with a small slice of the population at the top of the social pyramid. Within the working class of society, being a craftsman like Jesus was somewhere in the middle, along with teachers, lawyers, shopkeepers, fishermen, and farmers with their own land. This wasn't anything like a modern middle class—which has no real parallel in the ancient Mediterranean world—but Jesus's family would have been better off than many people who lived in abject poverty, such as slaves, tenant farmers, shepherds, and day laborers.[5] Above Jesus's family would have been wealthy merchants and the rich elite who inherited their wealth or gained it through political maneuvering.

This means that Jesus and his family could always see people who were better off economically and people who were worse off. Like us, he may have been tempted to envy the comfortably wealthy or overlook those who were struggling at social levels beneath his own.

UNDER CONSTRUCTION

One intriguing element of Jesus's work life goes unmentioned in the New Testament but was a significant factor for anyone in his line of work in Galilee at the time: the building of the city Sepphoris. That name may be unfamiliar because of its absence in the pages of Scripture, but during Jesus's lifetime Sepphoris became one of the best-known cities in the region, the so-called jewel of Galilee.[6]

Herod the Great ruled over the Jews on behalf of Rome at the time of Jesus's birth. His son Herod Antipas was the local ruler of Galilee during Jesus's working years. The building of Sepphoris was one of Antipas's most ambitious projects, and he dedicated the city to the Roman emperor.[7] The wealthy city became a hub of culture and commerce in the region and featured a theater that could seat over four thousand spectators, a miles-long aqueduct, and exquisite Greco-Roman works of art including intricate mosaics adorning pricey villas.[8]

Not only was this prominent city under construction during Jesus's working years; Sepphoris was only a few miles away from his hometown of Nazareth.

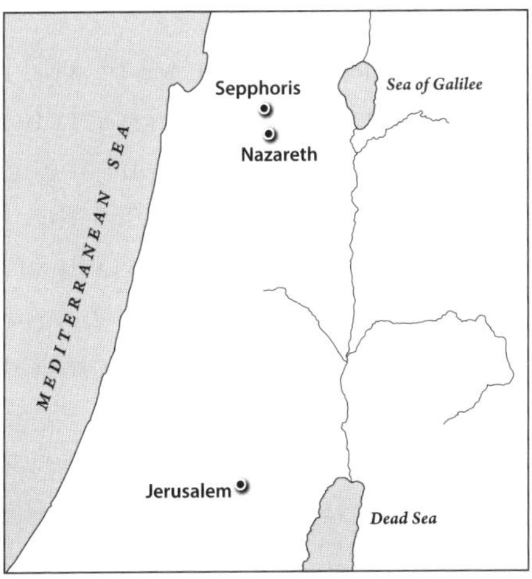

Considering the labor required to construct the streets, structures, and public works in and around an eminent city like Sepphoris, it is hard to imagine that experienced local craftsmen like Joseph, Jesus, and his brothers wouldn't have been involved in the project. Perhaps the government or wealthy residents looking to construct or decorate their villas contracted them. Jesus's family may have visited Sepphoris over the years for nonwork reasons like shopping, visiting friends, or even taking in a performance at the theater.[9]

Sepphoris was a glimmering symbol of Roman political, economic, and cultural power, and a tribute by Herod Antipas to Caesar, who was revered by many Romans as a god. The city was also full of imagery from the Greco-Roman pantheon of gods and goddesses. Assuming that Jesus worked occasionally in Sepphoris, he would have come face-to-face with imperial power and Greco-Roman paganism. His values and vision of the world may have been at odds with some of his employers. This is not to suggest that Jesus personally built anything idolatrous. I think it's safe to assume he would have declined explicitly pagan projects. But Jesus probably worked in and around Sepphoris—and other Gentile cities—whose worldviews were far from biblical.

Many of us have had the experience of working a job we don't love, reporting to a boss we don't especially like, or serving an organization whose values are out of alignment with our own. Jesus must have understood what that was like. He might have built homes for people whose lifestyles were far from godly. He may have been paid by the government to build structures that featured imperialistic pro-Roman motifs. But Jesus's job was to build things, and only so many projects were within walking distance of his home. He had to eat and help provide for his large family, even if some of his work was less than ideal.

OUR EVERYDAY MOMENTS

By now we have a mental sketch of Jesus's work life. He labored in the family trade, following in Joseph's footsteps. His brothers probably did too. Jesus worked as a craftsman for two decades before exchanging his trade and tools for sermons and miracles. His line of work required constant effort to generate new business, which added an arduous mental and emotional layer to work that was physically demanding. His commissions would have often come from neighbors and other people familiar to him, and he would have been paid occasionally by wealthy patrons—both private and governmental—in the construction of their opulent neighborhoods. As a craftsman, Jesus and his family were somewhere in the middle of a mostly poor society. Socially speaking, Jesus could look upward toward the wealthy and downward toward the hopelessly impoverished.

Jesus was tested in all ways like we are. As we navigate our often-strenuous work lives, we can go to him with confidence knowing that he truly understands. We should also remember that our work isn't our ultimate source of purpose, self-worth, or meaning; our work is a gift given to us by our creator, the meaning maker.

Jesus worked with his father and brothers. That was a blessing, I'm sure, but there's no question that there were frustrations working that closely and consistently with family. There was a customer service aspect to his work life too. Some of his customers would have been happy with his work; others would have complained. If you have experienced annoyance with coworkers, fellow volunteers, or customers, you can take that to Jesus each day, or even moment by moment, confident that he understands and that he will give you the wisdom and patience you need.

Jesus worked as a craftsman for two decades. We can assume

he did not find it equally interesting during all those years. There would have been projects that were more stimulating than others and opportunities that were more mundane and perhaps even boring. If you have felt a seasonality in your work satisfaction, Jesus probably experienced something similar. You can talk to him about it. Don't be concerned about whether your dissatisfaction will disappoint him; just be honest and ask him to shape your thoughts and mature your heart about your work life.

Sometimes we don't feel free to unplug after work, especially since many of us can take our work with us wherever we go thanks to our phones. If you have felt the inability to disengage from work or the constant need to develop new opportunities, Jesus understands. His work involved the perpetual entrepreneurial pursuit of building and sustaining his business. If you're a caregiver or stay-at-home parent and feel that the needs of those in your care never sleep, Jesus understands that kind of unrelenting work. You can pray about your own experience or be a listening ear and prayerful friend to someone else dealing with this kind of exhaustion.

Socially, if you feel that your career puts you somewhere in the middle of the pack, Jesus knows how that feels. If you can point to people in your life who seem to have it easy financially and you have to fend off envy, Jesus did that too. If you can point to people in your life who are struggling financially and you have to cultivate compassion and generosity toward them, Jesus knows what that is like.

If your employers have an organizational vision or leadership culture that you find bothersome or out of sync with your own values, Jesus lived that too. He understands the self-control and patience required and will help you.

Jesus had a work life, and the closer we examine it, the more relatable it seems. As we go about our own work lives, which are mostly routine, we should feel a sense of God's presence with us—not in some vague, theoretical sense but in a real, palpable sense, like a good friend sitting in the passenger seat, listening and sympathetically nodding along.

QUESTIONS FOR GROUP DISCUSSION OR PERSONAL REFLECTION

- What surprised or challenged you about this chapter?
- Of all the jobs Jesus could have done during his time on earth, why do you think building is the kind of work that he did?
- How do you see your own work life reflected in Jesus's occupation?
- In what ways do you need to trust Jesus with your work life?
- What is one step you can take this week to have a healthier relationship with your work?
- If you could ask Jesus something about your work and get an audible answer right now, what would you ask and why?

Dear Jesus, help me to have a proper view of my work life. Help me to remember that you experienced some of the same stresses that I go through, and you understand when I'm feeling pressure, exhaustion, or disillusionment. I don't have to hide my work life from you; I can entrust it to you. I don't have to expect my work to tell me that I'm valuable. You have already done that. Thank you for giving me my work; please also give me your heart about my work. Amen.

3

A Precarious Physical Life

When I was in kindergarten, we shared a duplex with a young family of four who experienced a terrible tragedy. One day, the husband and father went to work and didn't come home. He was killed in a freak accident at the construction site where he worked, leaving behind his immigrant wife who was still learning English and their two young children. Their sadness and disorientation made an impression on me. It's hard to forget our first encounter with human frailty.

My eighth-grade English teacher was one of the best I ever had. I still think of her grammatical instruction when I write and her impassioned literary analysis when I reread books that I first encountered in her class. Midway through the next year, ninth grade, I heard the heartbreaking news that she died unexpectedly due to complications from childbirth. I recall seeing classmates and sports teammates known for their toughness openly weeping at her funeral.

Ashley and I have watched our children face the realities of human frailty too. They once saw a woman who had no hands working at a grocery store. They talked about that for weeks and still mentioned it occasionally months and years later. They have lost two great-grandparents and saw their bodies at the funeral services. Recently they absorbed the news that a family friend, who was the same age as me, died of cancer.

In the news and in our personal lives, we are confronted daily with the fragility of human life and health. Even in our modern world with its accelerating advances in medical care, so many things must go right with our bodies for a long and healthy life to be possible. Of course, many people around the world today are born into families or communities where they cannot access quality medical care or maintain a healthy lifestyle, and they are in a much more unstable position than many of us. This would have been true for Jesus's family too, and for nearly everyone in the ancient world. Their physical lives were precarious. Let's consider this aspect of Jesus's life.

JESUS GREW UP

When God sent his Son to rescue humanity, he could have sent him fully grown. But he didn't. The Son of God wasn't beamed down to Earth's surface as in a scene from Star Trek; he was born like the rest of us. This means that Jesus experienced the mostly forgotten stresses of infancy. He cried when he was hungry or sick. He spit up. He protested naps and struggled to sleep through the night. He felt frustrated when learning to crawl, walk, and talk. After Joseph and Mary brought newborn Jesus for his dedication at the Jerusalem temple, Luke tells us that "they returned to Galilee to their own town of Nazareth. And the child grew and became strong" (Luke 2:39–40). Let's not miss the fact that Luke tells us Jesus "became" strong, implying that he was not strong before that. In his youngest years, Jesus was a helpless, vulnerable child, just like us.

And Jesus experienced being a teenager, with its attendant awkwardness and array of physical and emotional changes. Only one moment from Jesus's adolescent years is recorded in the New Testament, and it's found in Luke's gospel. When Jesus was twelve years old, his family took a trip from Nazareth down to Jerusalem for the Passover festival. This was the well-known occasion when Jesus's parents lost track of him and eventually found him conversing with the religious leaders in the temple. After this incident, Luke tells us that "Jesus grew in wisdom and stature" (2:52). The Greek word translated as "stature" can refer to physical height but also more broadly to maturity.[1] Jesus grew in wisdom, height, and maturity. Again, Luke highlights the obvious yet overlooked fact that Jesus grew up. He didn't appear on earth fully formed.

When I was a kid, I experienced recurring growing pains in my shins. I can remember how they felt and how sometimes it was hard to sleep because of them. I can also recall the emotional growing pains that are common to adolescence: a strong desire for freedom and independence, my social life taking center stage, and a newfound interest in girls at school. As a parent, I'm now watching my son enter this formative season of life. Jesus would have experienced these changes too as he grew up. He would have felt elation, embarrassment, attraction, social clumsiness, and all the other normal feelings that rush in during those formative adolescent years.

THE LOSS OF LOVED ONES

As we discovered earlier, Jesus probably had six or seven siblings. We don't often think about Jesus coming from such a large family because there is so much emphasis on him, Mary, and Joseph in the birth narratives of Matthew and Luke. But the fact that Jesus had that many siblings is significant when considered against the backdrop of ancient life expectancies and rates of infant mortality. Dr. Lynn Cohick summarizes the grim reality:

> Many women died in childbirth, and many children died in infancy or early childhood. In a tender testimony to his wife, Titus Julius Fortunatus, a Roman centurion, speaks of her incomparable nature and exceptional devotion (pietas) to him. They married when she was eleven years old and their marriage lasted sixteen years, until her death at age twenty-seven. During that time, she had six pregnancies, but only one child lived to adulthood. This harsh statistic unfortunately reflects the norm. Even in the upper echelons of society, infant mortality and the mother's death in childbirth were frighteningly high. Death was no respecter of wealth or status; Julius Caesar's daughter, Julia, died while giving birth (54 BC). Rich and poor suffered alike, as evidenced by Cornelia, the mother of Tiberias and Gaius Graccus—of her twelve live births, only three, including the two infamous brothers, survived into adulthood.[2]

The average life expectancy of someone living in the first-century Roman world was around twenty-five years old, but that does not mean that most adults died by that age. The reason the average life expectancy was so low is that so many people died in infancy.[3]

Taking all of this into account, it is no stretch to assume that Jesus's family lost one or more children during childbirth or infancy. This was heartbreakingly normal for the era, and they certainly would have known neighbors and extended family members who lost young ones under similar circumstances.

In addition to the assumption that Jesus lost younger siblings, we know of some specific losses that he endured. His earthly father, Joseph, must have died during Jesus's formative years. In Matthew and Luke, Joseph is only present in the narratives about Jesus's youth. He is mentioned retrospectively in Mark and John, both of which omit descriptions of Jesus's upbringing. This leads most biblical scholars to assume that Joseph died at some point between Jesus's adolescence and the beginning of his ministry, during those years when Jesus worked as a craftsman. Jesus, as the eldest son, would have had to bear not only the grief of losing Joseph but also additional family and social responsibilities as head of the household. We know too that Jesus lost his dear friend Lazarus to a fatal illness, a loss so severe that he publicly wept (John 11:35).

In the past several years, I lost a longtime family friend to COVID and another to a sudden heart attack in his early forties. I lost an uncle to complications related to a lifelong struggle with alcohol. I've also lost several relatives to the more ordinary complications of aging. I'm sure you have similar stories to tell. Loss is never easy, and when we grieve these seismic disruptions in our lives, we can turn to Jesus for comfort.

NUTRITION AND ILLNESS

In addition to Jesus's experiences growing up and his encounters with loss, he also had to contend with the commonplace challenges of having a human body: nutrition and illness. There are many scenes in the Gospels that describe Jesus eating and sharing meals with others. He got hungry, and at times he had to look for food (Matthew 12:1; Mark 11:12). For a typical ancient person like Jesus, bread made up 50–75 percent of their daily diet, with the rest consisting mostly of fish, lentils, and produce. Regular meat consumption was mainly a practice of the wealthy.[4] Most ancient people had nothing even close to an optimal or consistent diet, a reality that is true for much of the world even today. This and the scarcity of clean water contributed to the many illnesses that Jesus observed and would have experienced himself. Analysis of dental and skeletal remains from the era prove that malnutrition was common and a root cause of many maladies.[5]

Jesus was surrounded by illness throughout his life, but perhaps more so after he began his public ministry. Once the word spread that he could work miracles, people in desperation brought him their ailing friends and family members. In Matthew, we glimpse the scope of this suffering: "Jesus went throughout Galilee, teaching in their synagogues, proclaiming the good news of the kingdom, and healing every disease and sickness among the people. News about him spread all over Syria, and people brought to him all who were ill with various diseases, those suffering severe pain, the demon-possessed, those having seizures, and the paralyzed; and he healed them" (4:23–24).

A survey of the diseases mentioned in the New Testament includes forms of paralysis, blindness, skin diseases, bowel disorders, and various mental afflictions.[6] These were the forms of physical fragility Jesus was exposed to, and for those experiencing them there was little access to medical care, which was rudimentary and laced with superstition.

OUR EVERYDAY MOMENTS

Jesus could have appeared as a grown-up and spent only a few years here on earth, but he didn't. He grew over three decades and experienced normal growing pains—both emotional and physical. He probably knew what it was like to lose a younger sibling, his father, Joseph, and most likely cousins or other acquaintances. If you have known the inexpressible grief of losing a child, walking through a miscarriage, or burying a young sibling, Jesus almost certainly experienced something similar. He and his family traversed the desolate landscape of loss, and he understands how you felt and still feel. Turn to him for comfort, but don't stop there: invite your brothers and sisters in Christ to enter this wing of your life. Allow them to help you through the dark valley.

Jesus's diet would have been unhealthy by modern standards of nutrition, and a sustainable source of food was not convenient or guaranteed. Illness was extremely common and ominous because it would likely lead to death or disability. Hunger, pain, illness, and death were common to his life and to the lives of those he cared about. When you hear about families who live with perpetual food insecurity—whether residents of your own community or in far-off places—remember that Jesus grew up a lot like the kids in those families. Allow this knowledge to stoke a fresh compassion in your heart, and ask God to show you ways that you can partner with local or international aid organizations to help those who have such needs.

My family recently moved to a new city, so we've been in the process of establishing care with new dentists and doctors. Today, on the same day I wrote the first draft of this chapter, I checked in for my introductory visit with a new primary care doctor. I completed the check-in process on my phone. I can't help but reflect on the immense differences between health care in my context and what ancient people like Jesus experienced. On the other hand, people get sick and die in the twenty-first century just like they did then. Illness and loss are as fundamental to the human experience today as they were in first-century Galilee.

When we encounter human frailty in ourselves or others, we can turn to our Lord who remembers what it is like to experience pain, illness, and loss. He understands, and he invites us to trust him with our physical lives, which do often feel precarious. As David wrote in Psalm 103:3, the Lord heals all our diseases. This does not mean he heals every disease, of course, but rather *when* we are healed, it is because of his healing touch. And we who are in Christ will one day know life without the faintest trace of frailty.

QUESTIONS FOR GROUP DISCUSSION OR PERSONAL REFLECTION

- What surprised or challenged you about this chapter?
- What do you think about God when you experience illness or encounter it in someone else?
- How have you felt toward God when you've experienced loss?
- In what ways do you need to trust Jesus with your physical life and the lives of those you love?
- What is one step you can take this week to have a healthier outlook on your physical life?
- If you could ask Jesus something about your physical life and get an audible answer right now, what would you ask and why?

Dear Jesus, you created the human body, and you created my body. You know when my body is working well and when it's not. You've known every scratch and sniffle, every virus that's sickened me and the ones my immune system has protected me from. There is nothing my doctors know that is news to you, and you know much more about me than they could ever discover. You know when

I'm worried about my physical life and when I'm taking my health for granted. Help me to trust you with my physical life, comforted by the knowledge that you know how it feels to be human and that not one heartbeat escapes your notice. Amen.

4

A Criticized Public Life

Before the advent of social media, there were public figures and there were nonpublic figures. Now everyone can be a public figure, and many of us choose to be just that. As we share with the world in real time, there are positive outcomes: we cultivate friendships, connect with like-minded groups, and stay in touch with distant loved ones who we don't see on a regular basis. On the other hand, we can become consumed with curating our online personas, and we open ourselves up to the ever-scrutinizing eyes of people we know and far-off strangers we'll never meet.

This technological and relational reality intersects with an increasingly polarized society. When we have a negative shared experience like a natural disaster, war, pandemic, or divisive political season, it's challenging to find the goldilocks zone of healthy public dialogue. We're commenting too much online or too little. Leaders are either too heavy-handed or too hands-off. They're speaking out too much or not enough.

Jesus didn't inhabit this modern social and technological landscape, but his society was highly polarized too, which generated challenges similar to ours. When he first stepped out as a public figure after three decades of relative obscurity, he encountered the same criticisms that social media has brought into our lives. Depending on the audience, Jesus and his followers were sometimes viewed as too exclusive or not exclusive enough, too tolerant of Rome's occupation or not tolerant enough. Jesus was criticized by friends, family, and neighbors, and his message irritated spiritual and political leaders. He did not have a smartphone or social media, but Jesus was a traveling teacher. His words—repeated over and over by him and by his devotees—spread as rapidly and virally as words could in the ancient tinderbox of first-century Judea.

Let's consider three forms of criticism Jesus faced in his public life: criticism from those in his community, accusations that he went too far in his teachings, and opposite assertions that he was not going far enough.

CRITICISM CLOSE TO HOME

At the outset of Jesus's ministry, he was tempted in the wilderness by Satan. After that experience, he went to his hometown to officially move from a nonpublic person to a public figure. Luke records the moment: "Jesus returned to Galilee in the power of the Spirit, and news about him spread through the whole countryside. He was teaching in their synagogues, and everyone praised him. He went to Nazareth, where he had been brought up, and on the Sabbath day he went into the synagogue, as was his custom" (Luke 4:14–16).

Jesus participated in a typical synagogue service on that day, but it quickly became atypical when he claimed to be the fulfillment of Old Testament prophecy. Initially, the congregation was with him: "All spoke well of him and were amazed at the gracious words that came from his lips" (v. 22). But the muttering began instantly: "'Isn't this Joseph's son?' they asked." Jesus responded by stating that God's prophets had long been rejected by their own people, and that the Gentiles would welcome the good news. This maddened the crowd: "All the people in the synagogue were furious when they heard this. They got up, drove him out of the town, and took him to the brow of the hill on which the town was built, in order to throw him off the cliff. But he walked right through the crowd and went on his way" (vv. 28–30).

It's important that we understand who made up this "crowd." In many moments of Jesus's ministry, the crowd was full of people he didn't know who came from far away to hear his words and seek healing. But this crowd was different. This criticism that culminated in violent opposition came from people Jesus knew well. This was a synagogue service in his hometown, the kind of worship service he had attended hundreds of times over his life. These were not strangers; they were his friends and neighbors who criticized and forcefully rejected him. Some were clients of his. That kind of personal and public condemnation must have been deeply painful, even if he expected it.

But the opposition didn't stop with friends and neighbors. Jesus also experienced criticism from his own family. We saw earlier that Jesus's unbelieving brothers taunted him about proving his identity to the world (John 7:3–5). In the gospel of Mark, we see that his whole family (perhaps with the exception of Mary) had misgivings about his growing ministry, feeling that things were getting out of hand: "Then Jesus entered a house, and again a crowd gathered, so that he and his disciples were not even able to eat. When his family heard about this, they went to take charge of him, for they said, 'He is out of his mind'" (3:20–21).

As the word about their brother spread and the crowds who followed him were growing in size and fervor, Jesus's family became uneasy. They tried to confront him and physically prevent him from continuing. They felt that they needed to rein in their unstable brother. Notice that they spoke of him in the third person: "He is out of his mind." This implies they were speaking to others in the community about Jesus. They were embarrassed by him and wanted people to know where they stood: they thought he was crazy, or at least they wanted others to *think* that they thought he was crazy. Imagine how painful that must have been for Jesus!

CRITICISM THAT JESUS WENT TOO FAR

The Jewish religious leaders of Jesus's day, mostly based in Jerusalem, objected to much of what Jesus said and did. In their minds, he was a dangerous innovator. Jesus took too many liberties with his teachings and practices. He had too few guardrails about whom he associated with. In a word, he was cavalier. A flyover of their objections reveals how they saw Jesus:

> This fellow is blaspheming! (Matthew 9:3)
>
> Why does your teacher eat with tax collectors and sinners? (Matthew 9:11)
>
> How is it that we and the Pharisees fast often, but your disciples do not fast? (Matthew 9:14)
>
> Why do your disciples break the tradition of the elders? They don't wash their hands before they eat! (Matthew 15:2)
>
> Why are you doing what is unlawful on the Sabbath? (Luke 6:2)
>
> Not only was he breaking the Sabbath, but he was even calling God his own Father, making himself equal with God. (John 5:18)

> Here you are, appearing as your own witness; your testimony is not valid. (John 8:13)

In the eyes of the Jewish religious authorities, Jesus had gone too far. He may have been an undeniable miracle worker, but his alleged blasphemy and flouting of tradition undermined any possible admiration they might have for his supernatural acts.

Pontius Pilate, the Roman governor who presided over Jesus's trial, also accused him of claiming too much about himself. Pilate was most interested in the rumors he had heard about Jesus's supposed political claims. The governor had little interest in the differences between Jesus's religious perspective and that of the Jewish leadership. In Pilate's eyes, they were merely squabbles over the finer points of Jewish theology. But any political and messianic claims that Jesus made were very interesting to a Roman official. During his trial, Jesus had this exchange with Pilate:

> Pilate then went back inside the palace, summoned Jesus and asked him, "Are you the king of the Jews?"
>
> "Is that your own idea," Jesus asked, "or did others talk to you about me?"
>
> "Am I a Jew?" Pilate replied. "Your own people and chief priests handed you over to me. What is it you have done?"
>
> Jesus said, "My kingdom is not of this world. If it were, my servants would fight to prevent my arrest by the Jewish leaders. But now my kingdom is from another place."
>
> "You are a king, then!" said Pilate.
>
> Jesus answered, "You say that I am a king. In fact, the reason I was born and came into the world is to testify to the truth. Everyone on the side of truth listens to me." (John 18:33–37)

Pilate must have been surprised to hear Jesus claim that he had a kingdom somewhere. This alleged criminal standing before him, rejected by his own people's leaders, did not seem like any king Pilate had ever heard of. You can almost hear his incredulity and sarcasm when he said to Jesus, "You are a king, then!" He wasn't sure who Jesus was and didn't fully grasp the claims Jesus was making, but Pilate understood that whatever they were, Jesus was claiming too much. He had gone too far.

And of course, Satan, during Jesus's temptation in the wilderness, tried to plant the seed in Jesus's mind that he had gone too far. "If you are the Son of God . . ." he said more than once (Matthew 4:3, 6), perhaps with the emphasis on "if." His criticism of Jesus hinted that he thought too highly of himself, and his mission was misguided. Of course, this was a lie and Satan knew it, but it was the ugliest, most evil criticism that Jesus experienced. With the Spirit's help, Jesus endured the temptation and embarked on his public ministry.

CRITICISM THAT JESUS DIDN'T GO FAR ENOUGH

On the other end of the continuum, some felt that Jesus had a responsibility to say and do more than he already was—to give his spiritual message of freedom a more immediate, political edge. One group who probably felt this way were the Zealots, a social and political group of first-century Jews who coalesced and organized in the decades before, during, and after Jesus's life. The Zealots wished for Jewish religious renewal and were ardent advocates for independence from Rome. Their efforts escalated during the first century, and eventually enough Jews shared their sentiments that the nation rebelled against Rome a few decades after Jesus's life.[1]

One of Jesus's twelve disciples was known as Simon the Zealot.[2] He may or may not have been officially affiliated with the Zealots, but for him to have that nickname reported consistently in the New Testament means that his social and political perspectives must have trended toward the revolutionary.[3] People with this perspective were looking for a militaristic messiah and would most likely have felt that Jesus was not going far enough. He was too accommodating of the unjust, ungodly power structures of the day. In John's gospel, we learn that some people—probably of the Zealot persuasion—tried to compel Jesus to do more. John describes the scene immediately following Jesus's miraculous feeding of the five thousand: "After the people saw the sign Jesus performed, they began to say, 'Surely this is the Prophet who is to come into the world.' Jesus, knowing that they intended to come and make him king by force, withdrew again to a mountain by himself" (6:14–15). Jesus was not interested in becoming the kind of king they wanted, so they tried to force him to become one. In their minds, Jesus had not gone far enough.

OUR EVERYDAY MOMENTS

If you often feel as if you're being pulled in two directions—like you should either calm down or rev up—you're not alone. Many of us feel that way, and Jesus certainly did. He must have felt like that every day during his ministry. He was scrutinized by those who were closest to him and criticized by groups on opposite ends of the social spectrum who wanted him to become more or less extreme. To those who wanted him to take power, he demurred. To those who expected him to back down, he stood firm.

I once experienced a painful conflict in my extended family. I tried to stay as impartial as possible and facilitate a resolution, but ultimately both camps became upset that I wasn't taking a firmer stance and agreeing with their perspective. Mercifully, reconciliation happened, and that wound has become a painless scar, a fading memory. But that unpleasant feeling of being pulled in two directions was palpable at the time.

Have you ever been criticized by a friend or family member, like Jesus was? Maybe you shared something heartfelt on social media, and someone close to you felt compelled to disagree with you publicly, just so everyone would know where they stood. They took what you said and made it about them. Or maybe you shared your opinion about something personal with a group of coworkers and someone pushed back harder than you expected anyone would. Doesn't it hurt when people do that? That happened to Jesus too.

Have you ever been critiqued for doing something you thought was good? Maybe you've volunteered as a Little League coach or donated your time to a service project at your church or a local nonprofit. Maybe you've served on a committee at your kids' school. Whatever it is, have you ever given of yourself for the good of others and then been told you're doing it wrong? Community criticism, whatever its form, stings, because the negative feedback hits close to home. Jesus went through the same thing.

Has anyone ever made you feel like you're too serious about your faith? They act surprised when they find out you go to church every week, and they shift uncomfortably in their chair or break eye contact when you share about your spiritual life or offer to pray for them. It's obvious they feel your religion takes up too much space in your life or is intruding into theirs. Or maybe someone has suggested that your faith in Christ is anti-intellectual, or anachronistic, or quaint in the twenty-first century. Your faith has gone too far, they imply.

Or perhaps, sadly, a church leader has made you feel this way. Like you need to stay in your lane. You're trying to lead too much, take too much initiative. You're undermining their singular vision for the church's future. You've gone too far. Jesus understands how this feels. He was made to feel the same way.

We Christians feel guilty much more of the time than we probably should. Much of this guilt is shoveled onto us by other Christians who accuse us of not being serious enough about our faith. We're not zealous enough. We're not pushing back enough against the culture. Have you ever been made to feel that way? Maybe you've experienced this in the realm of politics. By supporting this political party or standing on the wrong side of this or that issue, you're not sufficiently standing up for God (as if he is actually vulnerable and needs you to defend him).

Or maybe you've felt this in your family life. You have family members who are making sinful life choices, and you've been made to feel that if you're too compassionate or loving toward them, then you're not being faithful to God. You're not standing up for the truth or what is right. You haven't gone far enough. Jesus felt some of those same things.

Perhaps you have made other Christians feel guilty about not being serious enough about their faith. If you have, and someone comes to mind, consider reaching out to them. Apologize if necessary, and help them to see that there is no condemnation in Christ and that they don't have to prove themselves to you or anyone else.

We've all faced criticism in our lives. Some of it is unfair, like the criticisms Jesus experienced. He was innocently misunderstood by some people and deliberately misunderstood by others. That hurts, and we need his help forgiving people who treat us that way. As a first step toward forgiveness, try making a list of ways you've been unfairly criticized over the years, and begin asking Jesus to help you forgive those who have hurt you. If you need to initiate reconciliatory conversations, ask for his help with that too; he'll give you the wisdom and grace you need.

But unlike Jesus's experience, we sometimes deserve the

criticism we receive. This is fair criticism—the kind that results from our own foolishness. Even when it's our fault, criticism is still hard to accept, especially when it comes from those we love or respect. Try adding a second column to your list of criticisms—a column devoted to criticism you've deserved. What can you do to turn things around or repair whatever you've damaged?

And let's not forget our silent self-criticism, which tends to blare the loudest.

Whatever the criticism and whoever the critic, Jesus isn't looking to join the stone throwers. His desire is to heal us from unfair criticism, grow us through fair criticism, and silence our inner antagonist by reminding us of who we are in his eyes—the eyes of the one who made us and loves us exponentially more than anyone else has ever loved us.

QUESTIONS FOR GROUP DISCUSSION OR PERSONAL REFLECTION

- What surprised or challenged you about this chapter?
- Why do you think it's so painful to experience public criticism?
- Have you been made to feel like you're going too far in your spiritual life? What was that like?
- Have you been made to feel like you're not going far enough? How would you describe that experience?
- What's something you can pray for when you criticize yourself?
- What is one step you can take this week to have healthier public relationships?
- If you could ask Jesus something about the criticism you've experienced and get an audible answer right now, what would you ask and why?

Dear Jesus, I was well aware of the criticism you faced from the Pharisees and other religious leaders, but I haven't always considered the other difficult elements of your public life. It comforts me to know that when I'm criticized, I can tell you about it and you really do know how it feels. As you loved those who publicly criticized and rejected you, please help me to have the right attitude toward those who say hurtful and critical things to me. My temptation is to write them off or vilify them in my heart, and I don't want to do that. Give me the desire and the ability to forgive. Thank you for always listening to my prayers, and for your love that never quits. Amen.

5

An Elusive Private Life

We in the twenty-first century have an uneasy relationship with privacy. Most of us, regardless of where we fall on the introvert-extrovert continuum, would say that we prize our privacy. Whether we want a lot of it or a little, we feel that privacy should be readily available to us, like turning on the faucet or switching on a light. As we explored in the previous chapter, our public lives can sometimes be challenging to bear, especially if we feel overly scrutinized or unfairly criticized. These kinds of experiences might be remedied by the pursuit of privacy, but that pursuit is not simple.

External factors rob us of privacy. With our ever-present phones in our pockets, our friends and family can always reach us. We rarely let a call or message go unanswered when they come to us from someone we care about. There's nothing wrong, of course, with being able to stay in touch with our loved ones in real time, but privacy pays the price. For many modern people, this happens on a professional level too. We never really leave the office, whether or not we work in an actual office. We can take much of our work along with us wherever we go. There are benefits to this flexibility, but a consequence is that we are always on call, which leads to a perpetual sense of busyness. Whether it's work or friends, the incoming signals rarely take a break.

But that's only half the challenge. We actively rob ourselves of privacy too. The truth is that our uneasy relationship with privacy is largely self-inflicted. We want privacy, but we fail to keep external threats to solitude at bay, and we pilfer whatever pockets of privacy we have left. When we do have a time of solitude or a private moment with a loved one or small group of friends, we feel an urge to make it public: post it, share it, comment on it, document it. Many of our private moments have become potential—or perhaps inevitable—public moments. It's almost as if private moments have lost their meaning; they must be broadcast to others in order to feel significant to us.

There is also the ongoing societal concern that our personal information is being monitored, stored, and in many cases sold by the companies that created our phones and the various technology platforms that have woven themselves into our lives. This makes us wonder, even if subconsciously, how possible it is to keep anything private anymore.

Jesus did not have a smartphone, and life in first-century Galilee was much less frenetic than our own. But he lived in a crowded, possibly multigenerational home in a tight-knit community. Personal space may have been less available than in our modern lives. Jesus had to fight for whatever privacy and solitude was possible in his historical context. It was a personal priority for him, and because of his stature as a public figure, people and pressures constantly tried to rob him of privacy. We can learn much by following his example.

During his ministry, Jesus sought out places the gospel writers called *erēmos*, an ancient Greek word for remote geographic locales where one could feel removed. The term is variously translated into English as "desert" or "wilderness," or a place that is "desolate" or "solitary."[1] In first-century Judea and Galilee, it wasn't difficult to find solitary places or deserts. Jesus, an increasingly public figure, sought out these desolate places. Sometimes he did so proactively; sometimes he isolated himself as a reaction to something heavy that happened. He sought seclusion for personal reasons, because of the ever-clutching crowds, and because of specific people or groups who were endangering his ministry. Let's consider a few examples of when Jesus pursued privacy.

SOLITARY PLACES

The gospel of Luke records an interaction between Jesus and a man who had leprosy. The man, knowing what Jesus was capable of, found him in one of the towns and begged for healing. He said to Jesus, "Lord, if you are willing, you can make me clean" (5:12). Jesus told him that he was willing and touched the man, saying, "Be clean!" (v. 13). At that moment, the leprosy became a memory. Jesus cautioned the man about telling too many people about what had happened, but these life-altering miracles did not stay secret for long. As Luke describes it, "The news about [Jesus] spread all the more, so that crowds of people came to hear him and to be healed of their sicknesses. But Jesus often withdrew to lonely places and prayed" (vv. 15–16).

These lonely places, where Jesus could find some peace and quiet to think and pray, were often found early in the morning. Mark tells us that "very early in the morning, while it was still dark, Jesus got up, left the house and went off to a solitary place, where he prayed" (Mark 1:35). Luke corroborates that this was Jesus's practice and explains why he availed himself of the dawn solitude: "At daybreak, Jesus went out to a solitary place. The people were looking for him and when they came to where he was, they tried to keep him from leaving them" (Luke 4:42).

It was challenging for Jesus to simultaneously serve the

growing crowds while also protecting his ability to have secluded moments and quieter times with his inner circle to rest, reflect, and plan. Mark provides a window into this situation:

> Because so many people were coming and going that [the apostles] did not even have a chance to eat, he said to them, "Come with me by yourselves to a quiet place and get some rest."
>
> So they went away by themselves in a boat to a solitary place. But many who saw them leaving recognized them and ran on foot from all the towns and got there ahead of them. (Mark 6:31–33)

The picture that emerges from the Gospels is that the more public Jesus's life became, the more intentional he was about retreating from it. The inescapable celebrity that followed in the wake of his miracles and sermons required him to be ever more intentional about finding quiet times and spaces, even as he sought to engage more and more people with his life-changing message. Prayer was a vital part of his spiritual life, and uninterrupted communion with his Father was something he fought for.

SPACE FOR PAIN

At other times Jesus sought out solitude not because of the ongoing demands of the crowds but because of painful experiences or the negative behavior of others. When he felt big feelings—sadness, loss, anger, fear—he knew that he needed to retreat. Just like us, he had to face how he felt and prayerfully work through it.

For example, when John the Baptist was murdered, the loss of his relative and friend affected Jesus deeply. He took a boat and quietly paddled toward solitude. He sought out private time to pray and to process. He may have stayed in the boat, drifting aimlessly around the Sea of Galilee, or he may have taken the boat to a secluded cove or a less populous shore of the lake. Matthew describes what Jesus did and explains that the solitude was short-lived because of the crowds who were constantly searching for him:

> John's disciples came and took his body and buried it. Then they went and told Jesus.
>
> When Jesus heard what had happened, he withdrew by boat privately to a solitary place. Hearing of this, the crowds followed him on foot from the towns. When Jesus landed and saw a large crowd, he had compassion on them and healed their sick. (14:12–14)

ESCAPE FROM ANTAGONISM

Jesus also sought out solitude because of threats from people who were not supportive of his mission and message, or who misunderstood him. As we read earlier in the gospel of John, some of the crowds had misguided motives for following Jesus. On the heels of an especially astounding miracle, they declared, "Surely this is the Prophet who is to come into the world" (6:14). But Jesus knew how their hearts were mistaken: "Jesus, knowing that they intended to come and make him king by force, withdrew again to a mountain by himself" (v. 15).

These crowds were pushing Jesus to take his ministry in a political direction and intended to use him for their own ends. He retreated again, this time to a higher elevation. Perhaps while Jesus was up there, presumably praying, he remembered another mountaintop experience: Satan tempting him with the same type of earthly political power (Matthew 4:8–9). His response to Satan was to quote Scripture. Maybe Jesus was doing the same thing when the crowd tried to make him king: he found a quiet place to pray, recite the Scriptures, and remind himself of what was true about his Father and his mission.

In the aftermath of another profound miracle—the raising of Lazarus—a powerful group plotted to thwart Jesus's ministry by taking his life. Again, Jesus's strategy was to retreat to a less populous area: "So from that day on they plotted to take his life. Therefore Jesus no longer moved about publicly among the people of Judea. Instead he withdrew to a region near the wilderness, to a village called Ephraim, where he stayed with his disciples" (John 11:53–54). Jesus realized that the remedy for misguided or malicious crowds was strategic retreat. He sought out solitude and privacy with smaller groups of close friends and followers.

OUR EVERYDAY MOMENTS

Jesus needed solitude and practiced privacy. He did this, it seems, to have a right view of himself, of his Father, and of his purpose. As we've seen, Jesus had to fight for it. Left unattended, his whole life would have become irreversibly public because of his increasing notoriety. His prayer life would have limped along, and he would have struggled to bear the burdens of those pursuing him—people whose intentions ranged from the benignly misguided to the malicious.

Jesus needed to, and did, find solitary places to pray and reflect. His experiences, unique as they were, have some parallels in our modern lives. Parents of young children know how it feels to always be on, to never have a break, to constantly be needed, and to find privacy elusive. The cumulative exhaustion of constant availability takes its toll, and alone time becomes a treasure when it can be unearthed. Just as Jesus felt a tension between serving the crowds and protecting his privacy, parents often feel the tension of wanting to spend quality time with their children while also needing space to think, pray, and rest. Many parents feel this tension at the beginning of summer vacation. We're glad to see more of our kids, but we feel apprehensive about the loss of personal time that came more easily during the school year. These mixed feelings are not unlike what Jesus probably experienced.

We get the same sensations from social media. If we want to, we can offer up a feed of our lives so everyone we've ever known is aware of and commenting on what we're sharing. With such a public life, which constantly demands to be fed, times of prayer and reflection can feel forever just beyond our fingertips. Have we given everyone we know a key to every room of our lives, or have we reserved some spaces for just ourselves and maybe a few close loved ones? We should follow Jesus's example of seeking out those solitary places, and we should be more vigilant about it—not less—the more public our lives become.

Jesus also cleared room for himself when he went through something acutely painful. If you've ever experienced a shattering loss or wandered through a bleak emotional wilderness, Jesus felt those things too. Just as you needed support from friends but also space for quiet moments of crying and reflecting, Jesus needed those things too.

He also, at times, moved out of earshot of his antagonists. Maybe you have experienced something challenging along these lines. Perhaps there's someone who won't leave you alone, whether it's an online troll, an antagonistic neighbor, or a jealous colleague. You just want to go on with your life or your work, but someone in your world is oddly committed to bothering you. If you've battled something like that, remember that Jesus did too. He confronted antagonists on many occasions, but on others he distanced himself from their voices. You may need to take similar steps in your life, whether it's sharing less of yourself on social media, becoming less responsive to messages, or allowing an irritating or intrusive relationship to naturally fade away.

If Jesus felt the need to nourish a private life and guard it from the public, we would be wise to do the same. To have a right view of ourselves, of others, and of God, we need solitude, and we have to fight for it. We must learn to be still and know God as he is (Psalm 46:10).

In our often antsy and anxious lives, carving out regular intervals of solitude can feel impossible. It is possible, though, if we're willing to be deliberate about it. Consider the words of Henry David Thoreau, in the opening paragraphs of his seminal work *Walden*: "When I wrote the following pages, or rather the bulk of them, I lived alone, in the woods, a mile from any neighbor, in a house which I had built myself, on the shore of Walden Pond, in Concord, Massachusetts, and earned my living by the labor of my hands only. I lived there two years and two months."[2]

Feeling the frantic crush of modernity closing in around him, Thoreau decisively retreated into a simpler life. He sought privacy. Most of us don't require two years in the woods to feel the healing effects of seclusion, but we do need times of solitude to be healthy, and such times won't come to us passively. In the words of Henri Nouwen,

> A life without a lonely place, that is, a life without a quiet center, easily becomes destructive. . . . In solitude we can listen to the voice of him who spoke to us before we could speak a word, who healed us before we could make any gesture to help, who set

us free long before we could free others, and who loved us long before we could give love to anyone. It is in this solitude that we discover that being is more important than having, and that we are worth more than the results of our efforts.[3]

QUESTIONS FOR GROUP DISCUSSION OR PERSONAL REFLECTION

- What surprised or challenged you about this chapter?
- Why do you think a private life is so difficult to achieve and maintain?
- In what ways can you prioritize solitude in your life?
- What's something you can pray for when your life feels too public?
- What is one step you can take this week to have a healthier relationship with privacy?
- If you could ask Jesus something about your private life and get an audible answer right now, what would you ask and why?

Dear Jesus, I want to want solitude. Sometimes I do want it, but often it doesn't occur to me to prioritize it until I'm stretched thin. I recognize that my prayer life suffers because of this tendency. Help me to know when it's wise to step back and spend time with you and with myself. Help me to be a spiritually and mentally healthy person. Please use private times in my life to bring about that health, and when you do, help me to recognize it and be thankful. Amen.

6

An Insecure Financial Life

Americans have a peculiar relationship with money. In a nation with arguably more wealth and financial opportunity than any in history, most of us—who are not actually impoverished—feel dissatisfied, unhappy, and fearful about money. On the one hand, we're consumed by the pursuit of wealth and enamored with conspicuous displays of it. On the other hand, we don't want to talk about our finances because we feel it's a private matter or too stressful to verbalize. Money is a source of tension and insecurity for millions of us.[1]

We are ever attentive to the whispered (and sometimes shouted) lie that money by itself can make us happy. There may be some truth to that, but only up to a point. A recent study concluded that peoples' happiness and overall well-being increases along with their annual income as it approaches the threshold where they can reliably afford to provide for their basic needs such as food, housing, and health care. However, levels of happiness begin to plateau for many people above that amount, regardless of how much more a person earns. In other words, their happiness does not continue to ascend in proportion to their income.[2]

Another recent study surveyed hundreds of individuals whose net worth is more than one million dollars. The respondents were asked to rate their happiness on a scale of 1 to 10, with 10 being the happiest. Then they were asked how much more money they would need to reach the maximum happiness level of 10. Many of the millionaire respondents answered that having two, five, or even ten times as much money would bring their happiness to the highest level of 10.[3]

Regardless of our income level, we want to be well provided for, and in an individualistic society such as ours, we want to do the providing ourselves. We feel ashamed if we must rely on others and balk at intrusions into our financial affairs like government taxation or unsolicited advice. We are not emotionally skilled at handling uncertainty, so we want our financial foundations to be rock-solid, able to weather unforeseen challenges and to prop up our spending habits. If any of these elements are out of calibration, we experience feelings of insecurity, fear, and inferiority. Against this anxious backdrop, Paul's words to Timothy are a critical corrective:

> Godliness with contentment is great gain. For we brought nothing into the world, and we can take nothing out of it. But if we have food and clothing, we will be content with that. Those who want to get rich fall into temptation and a trap and into many foolish and harmful desires that plunge people into ruin and destruction. For the love of money is a root of all kinds of evil. Some people, eager for money, have wandered from the faith and pierced themselves with many griefs. (1 Timothy 6:6–10)

This book is about Jesus's life, so what can we know about his relationship with money? What did he feel or experience in response to financial challenges? While there are many unknowable elements of his financial affairs, we do know a lot about economic conditions in the time and place where he lived. Jesus was not a modern Western person, and he did not embrace idolatrous views toward wealth. So, he would have felt somewhat differently about money than we do. But he did experience many of the same financial realities and pressure points, and as a human his emotional responses would certainly have overlapped with ours. Let's first consider his financial life prior to his public ministry and then consider his economic circumstances after he began traveling and teaching.

BEFORE HIS MINISTRY

Jesus's family was not rich. It's an arresting idea that Jesus did not choose a life of wealth and comfort during his time among us when he certainly could have arranged it. We know Jesus was not rich because he was a first-century Jew living in Galilee, which was not an especially affluent area compared to the rest of the Roman world. Much of Galilee was rural and rustic, and most people made their living in modest ways: farming, fishing, selling wares, and providing basic labor services. Galilee had some advantages economically, especially the fertile soil, an optimal location along trade routes, and a fishing industry connected to the Sea of Galilee. Judea, on the other hand, was a center of wealth and power because of Jerusalem, but it was less strategically located and the land itself was arid. Wealth could be found in Galilee too, as in all corners of the Roman Empire, but it was concentrated in ancestrally affluent families and those connected to the local power structures.

We have some specific insight from the New Testament into the economic circumstances of Jesus's family. After he was born, his parents brought him to Jerusalem for his purification and dedication. A sacrifice was to accompany the ceremonial practice. This moment in Jesus's life is described in Luke: "When the time came for the purification rites required by the Law of Moses, Joseph and Mary took him to Jerusalem to present him to the Lord (as it is written in the Law of the Lord, 'Every firstborn male is to be consecrated to the Lord'), and to offer a sacrifice in keeping with what is said in the Law of the Lord: 'a pair of doves or two young pigeons'" (2:22–24).

According to Luke, Mary and Joseph's sacrifice was rooted in an income-related regulation spelled out in Leviticus: "When the days of her purification for a son or daughter are over, she is to bring to the priest at the entrance to the tent of meeting a year-old lamb for a burnt offering and a young pigeon or a dove for a sin offering. . . . If she cannot afford a lamb, she is to bring two doves or two young pigeons, one for a burnt offering and the other for a sin offering. In this way the priest will make atonement for her, and she will be clean" (12:6, 8).

Luke tells us that's exactly what Mary and Joseph offered. Jesus's family could not afford to pay for the standard offering after his birth, so they paid for the less expensive offering. They offered what they could.

As we discovered in chapter 2, Jesus and his father, Joseph, were craftsmen. The family profession required entrepreneurial exertion and physical labor. Jesus's family would have been paid only when they were working, and their income would have covered their expenses for that period and little more. It appears they were not desperately poor, but if there was an ancient version of living paycheck to paycheck, Jesus's family was probably locked into that kind of financial rhythm.

Added to this, Jews of Jesus's day found themselves entangled in a web of heavy and capricious taxes, and they had no say in the matter. Whatever amount Jesus was able to earn, he could anticipate a sizable percentage of it going out the door to support corrupt and coercive governments. His family lived and labored under the threatening eyes of despots, both local and remote. The taxes he and his loved ones had to pay would have squeezed them financially even more than they already were, and would have been an unwelcome reminder of how the Jews had been dominated by greater political powers for centuries.

Taxation comes into view several times in the Gospels. Jesus befriended tax collectors such as Matthew and Zacchaeus, who were despised for their unpopular occupation. And Jesus was challenged repeatedly by his opponents on the propriety of paying state and temple taxes.[4] Taxation was an inescapable, burdensome part of life that caused division within the society where Jesus lived.

The lion's share of the taxes were paid to Rome and came in three primary forms: a direct tax demanded from every resident of the empire (*tributum capitis*), a tax on crops produced (*tributum soli*), and customs on goods moving through certain ports or trade routes (*portoria*).[5] There was also sales tax, inheritance tax, municipal taxes, and an annual temple tax. These taxes were paid to often crooked local officials who contracted with Rome to pay a certain amount in annual tribute but who collected much more than they were supposed to—pocketing the difference and enriching themselves. This seems to be the common but corrupt practice that Zacchaeus felt guilty about in his interaction with Jesus (Luke 19:8).

There's much we don't know about the finer points of Galilee's economics, but suffice it to say that poverty was prevalent, taxation was heavy, and wealth was concentrated in the hands of a few.

DURING HIS MINISTRY

Jesus's ministry was a traveling one. His home base seems to have been Capernaum (Matthew 4:13), but he was always on the move. He repeatedly crisscrossed Galilee and visited Judea to see friends and participate in religious festivals. It seems he was not working his usual job as a craftsman during this period, so how could Jesus afford to live? We know that he relied on the kindness of friends and strangers to provide food and lodging for him and his disciples. Luke highlights some of these providers: "After this, Jesus traveled about from one town and village to another, proclaiming the good news of the kingdom of God. The Twelve were with him, and also some women who had been cured of evil spirits and diseases: Mary (called Magdalene) from whom seven demons had come out; Joanna the wife of Chuza, the manager of Herod's household; Susanna; and many others. These women were helping to support them out of their own means" (Luke 8:1–3).

The fact that wealthy, politically connected women were providing financially for Jesus is an overlooked and underappreciated element of his ministry. These were key leadership roles played by women in a highly patriarchal culture. For some people at the time, their political connections may have opened Jesus up to cynical criticism by those who were looking to question his credentials and motives.

Even though Jesus had benefactors who made his full-time ministry possible, this does not mean he always had enough to eat or a roof over his head. I imagine he and his disciples had to sometimes hunt or fish for their food and on occasion sleep under the stars with growling stomachs. At one point, a teacher of the law came to Jesus and expressed his desire to follow him. Jesus replied, "Foxes have dens and birds have nests, but the Son of Man has no place to lay his head" (Matthew 8:20). He was letting this man know that if he really intended to follow him, he was signing up for an itinerant life with no expectation of comfortable accommodations.

OUR EVERYDAY MOMENTS

The idea that Jesus had a financial life might be new for you. I spent little time considering that fact for most of my life as a Christian. But now that we have a sense of his economic life, how does this deepen our intimacy with our savior?

If you have ever wished that you were born with a leg up financially or that you had grown up in a family with greater financial stability, Jesus knows what that is like. You can ask for him to help guard your heart against bitterness or jealousy toward those who seem to have it easy.

If you feel insecure because you think it's obvious to others that you're struggling financially, Jesus knows how that feels. His parents could not afford the standard sacrifice when he was born, and I'm sure that was just one of many instances when their hardship was evident. If the clothes you wear or the car you drive seem to advertise your financial need, you can ask Jesus to help you find your sense of worth in him instead of in your possessions, or in what others think about you.

If you feel stuck in a job that only pays enough for you to barely get by, Jesus understands. If your work feels contingent and inconsistent, he knows what that's like too. If you feel physically exhausted at the end of interminable work shifts that are taking you nowhere, you can rest assured that your savior ended some of his days with the same depleted sighs.

When you have to pay taxes, fork over money for unexpected fees, get overcharged for a service, or perhaps pay a speeding ticket or other fine that you feel is unfair, remember that Jesus and his family had similar experiences. They routinely saw rich tax collectors confiscate what little money they and their neighbors had sacrificed to accumulate. You can ask for Jesus's help when you're fuming over the unfairness, and for the grace to face your fears of being out of control.

If you've ever had to swallow your pride and ask for money from a friend or family member, Jesus knows how that feels too. His ministry relied on the generosity of others. When you feel embarrassed or criticized by what people say, post, or imply about your circumstances, Jesus remembers how it feels to have others talk about you like that.

On the other hand, if you have plenty of money but still go through life feeling afraid or envious about money, Jesus knew people like you when he was here on earth, and he loved them. He loves you too. He would counsel you to ask the Holy Spirit for the ability to trust in him instead of in your wealth, and he would encourage you to look around you for those in need. Help them, and God will begin to heal your heart. Jesus wants you to feel gratitude and contentment about your financial life, and generosity is the way to get there.

When your life feels wobbly, and you're nagged by a sense of uncertainty or lack of permanence, remember that Jesus spent his days traveling, often unsure of where he would sleep that night. You can ask him to ease your anxiety. Jesus was tested financially just as you have been and will continue to be, and he loves you more than you could possibly imagine.

QUESTIONS FOR GROUP DISCUSSION OR PERSONAL REFLECTION

- What surprised or challenged you about this chapter?
- What does it say about God that he chose a life that was financially insecure?
- In what ways do you need to trust Jesus with your financial life—whether you have an abundance or have little?
- Why do you think we struggle so much with how to handle money and how to feel about it?

- What is one step you can take this week to have a healthier relationship with your finances?
- If you could ask Jesus something about your finances and get an audible answer right now, what would you ask and why?

God, I confess that I often have a wrong view of my money. I elevate it to a higher place in my heart than I should. When I feel financially secure, I put too much trust in that money. When I feel financially insecure, I put too little trust in you. Please correct my heart's course when it comes to money. It's comforting to know, Jesus, that you had a financial life during your time on earth, and you understand what I feel. Help me to be a godly steward of my finances, and please bring people into my life who can guide me in my growth. Help me also, if I'm ready, to be a guide to others. I recognize that any financial resources I have are a gift from you. Thank you for all the ways you take care of me. Amen.

INTERLUDE

Joy, Understated

We're midway through our exploration of Jesus's ordinary human life, so let's catch our breath for a moment. We should recall Hebrews 4:15, that essential signpost at the beginning of our journey: "We do not have a high priest who is unable to empathize with our weaknesses, but we have one who has been tempted in every way, just as we are—yet he did not sin."

Remember that the word "tempted" in that verse really means "tested." Jesus was tested in every way, just as we are, so he can empathize with our weaknesses. We have seen several of the ways he was tested in the first part of this book: in his family life, work life, physical life, public life, private life, and financial life. There is much more to learn about his time on earth, but we've already covered a lot of ground, and hopefully you're beginning to see how many touchstones there are between Jesus's human experiences and your own. His were ancient experiences and yours are modern, but they're *human* experiences that transcend chronology.

Before we resume our journey, it's important to pause and acknowledge that most of what we're exploring in Jesus's human experiences is on the negative side of the ledger: the things that were a struggle for him. This is by design. Hebrews 4 tells us that Jesus was tested as we are. The focus is on elements of his and our lives that are challenging—our weaknesses. The pathos of life. So, we've been in a minor key.

But let's not imagine that Jesus was unhappy most of the time or that pain and toil were the dominant features of his life. Just as joy and difficulty mingle in our lives, so they did in Jesus's time on earth. Every one of us has to cultivate harbors of joy in the sometimes choppy waters of life, and we can assume that no one did this more successfully than Jesus, the son of God.

When we read the Gospels, we have to look for Jesus's happiness between the lines. The joy is there, but it doesn't always jump off the page. Much of the time it's offstage. Overheard. Around the corner. Hinted at. Implied. This is partly because of the formal literary style of the Gospels, which can make Jesus seem a bit stoic. It can also appear that his life was mainly a negative experience because the gospel writers focus on the final days of his life: his arrest, trial, and crucifixion.

But the entire purpose of Jesus's life was to come and lay it down for all of us, and it was love for us and joy that drove him to do that. As the author of Hebrews puts it: "For the joy set before him he endured the cross, scorning its shame, and sat down at the right hand of the throne of God" (12:2). The joy set before him was a reunion with humanity, an end to the estrangement between creator and created. All of Jesus's human life, despite its many difficulties, was infused with and driven by the joy of his rescue mission.

Jesus spoke about a shepherd searching for his lost sheep, and how when he finds it, "he joyfully puts it on his shoulders" (Luke 15:5). This is how Jesus felt when people responded to his gospel. The Holy Spirit helped to cultivate joy in Jesus's life too. After sending out seventy-two disciples to share the gospel, "Jesus, full of joy through the Holy Spirit, said, 'I praise you, Father, Lord of heaven and earth, because you have hidden these things from the wise and learned, and revealed them to little children. Yes, Father, for this is what you were pleased to do'" (10:21).

On the eve of Jesus's arrest, he spoke joyfully with his disciples: "As the Father has loved me, so have I loved you. Now remain in my love. If you keep my commands, you will remain in my love, just as I have kept my Father's commands and remain in his love. I have told you this so that my joy may be in you and that your joy may be complete" (John 15:9–11).

Praying to his heavenly Father on that same evening, Jesus said: "I am coming to you now, but I say these things while I am still in the world, so that they may have the full measure of my joy within them" (17:13).

Jesus's home life may have been mixed-up, but it was also full of joy. He had parents and younger siblings who loved him and whom he loved. He celebrated birthdays with them and laughed when they learned to walk and talk. He played with them.

Jesus's work life was strenuous, but it must have also been quite rewarding. I can imagine his satisfaction on completing a beautiful project in his neighborhood or in nearby Sepphoris. He would have felt encouraged when his clients smiled at a job well done.

Jesus's physical life was precarious, but he also seems to have made it to his early thirties without a permanently debilitating illness. This means that over the years he would have enjoyed footraces with his friends, playing sports, swimming, hiking, exploring, and all kinds of recreational activities.

He may have been criticized in public, but Jesus also met lots of new friends during his ministry and smiled at the lives being transformed in front of him.

He may have struggled to find private moments, but when

he did find them, Jesus must have taken deep breaths and enjoyed the tranquil beauty of creation and the gift of silence.

His financial life may have been insecure, but he must have also felt a deep sense of gratitude when he was paid for his work, thankful for the ability to provide for himself and his family.

Do we envision our savior coolly scowling his way through Galilee or warmly smiling among the crowds, with friends at his side? The latter is what we should imagine. The gospel writers may not have used the word *smile* to describe Jesus's demeanor, but he must have been smiling much of the time, especially in indisputably joyful moments:

> The kingdom of God has come near. Repent and believe the good news! (Mark 1:15)
>
> Let the little children come to me, and do not hinder them, for the kingdom of heaven belongs to such as these. (Matthew 19:14)
>
> He took her by the hand and said to her, "*Talitha koum!*" (which means "Little girl, I say to you, get up!") (Mark 5:41)
>
> Rejoice with me; I have found my lost sheep. (Luke 15:6)
>
> Lazarus, come out! . . . Take off the grave clothes and let him go. (John 11:43–44)

We're about to resume our journey, learning more about Jesus's human life, such as his emotions, culture, politics, social life, and spiritual life. Again, the focus will be on what was challenging, because we're exploring how Jesus was tested so that we can find comfort during our own times of testing. But let's keep the lesson of this interlude with us. Jesus's life was rooted in and driven by joy—the joy of a restored relationship with his most precious of creations: us.

7

A Heavy Emotional Life

Tales of adversity—whether fictional or factual—are some of the most compelling stories we know of. When we read the harrowing firsthand accounts of people like Solomon Northup, Corrie ten Boom, Helen Keller, or Anne Frank, we feel pulled into the crucible of their experiences. Our emotions resonate with what they felt.

Jesus had feelings too. He experienced the full range of human emotions. He certainly had many positive experiences and the feelings that come with them: joy over the birth of a younger sibling, happiness at spending time with friends and family, anticipation of celebrating holidays, satisfaction over a job well done, laughter at a well-timed joke. We have a sense of humor, so it goes without saying that our creator does as well!

But Jesus had unsettling experiences too and the heavy emotions that come along with them. These negative feelings undoubtedly influenced his teaching. Only someone who knew callousness and generosity could compose the parable of the good Samaritan. Only someone who knew ache and regret could author the parable of the prodigal son. Only someone who felt judgment and desperation could compose the parable of the Pharisee and the tax collector.

Jesus felt the things we all feel. He was able to give us such heartrending parables not only because of his divine omniscience but also because of his lived human experiences. Let's consider a few of the heavy feelings Jesus experienced and find comfort in knowing that he really understands how we feel.

ANNOYANCE

Adolescents have a knack for being annoyed. I remember feeling that way, and now that my children are entering that formative period in their lives, I'm reminded of what it was like. Jesus would have had the same proclivity in his youth. I believe we get a glimpse of this in the gospel of Luke in the well-known story of Mary and Joseph losing track of Jesus during a trip to Jerusalem. The account begins, "When [Jesus] was twelve years old . . ." (2:42). If you remember being a twelve-year-old or know anyone who is twelve, then you know there is a lot of information in that phrase. Jesus was experiencing a flurry of physiological, psychological, and emotional changes. He was a twelve-year-old. Not a monkish grown-up shrunk down to the size of a twelve-year-old. Jesus was actually twelve.

When we read the account of that family trip through the eyes of anyone who has ever been a parent, we find Mary and Joseph's exasperated comments to be highly relatable: "Son, why have you treated us like this? Your father and I have been anxiously searching for you" (v. 48). And when we read Jesus's response as the reply of an actual twelve-year-old, the annoyance jumps off the page: "'Why were you searching for me?' he asked. 'Didn't you know I had to be in my Father's house?'" (v. 49).

We tend to spiritualize this episode to such a degree that

all of Jesus's twelve-year-oldness is drained out of it. We read it as if Jesus is simply discipling his parents out of their faulty theology. Sure, there was some discipleship going on, and Jesus was an exceptionally gifted child, but I suspect there was also some normal, non-sinful annoyance too. Maybe even an eye roll. Jesus was an actual adolescent who was probably craving some freedom and independence. Like most kids his age, he probably wanted to be trusted by his parents with a little more responsibility. Maybe he had been looking forward to this family trip as an opportunity to roam a bit more freely and explore, and then felt frustrated at their attempts to rein him in.

Jesus is fully God and fully human, which means there was a year in world history when Jesus was fully twelve.

When my son was eleven years old, he started to want some space before and after his baseball games and practices. When dropping him off, I couldn't get too close to the dugout. When picking him up afterward, I needed to maintain a certain distance and let him come to me. One time I made the mistake of interrupting him when he was talking with his friends. I was in a hurry and needed him to pick up the pace so we could leave the ballpark. In the process I accidentally embarrassed him, and he was annoyed. I felt badly about it. As a kid, I remember feeling the same things toward my parents. Jesus was not a twenty-first-century American adolescent, but he must have felt a similar dynamic as he began to move from childhood toward adulthood.

I detect a faint trace of annoyance later in Jesus's life too. At a wedding, Jesus sat among friends, disciples, and family. He was enjoying himself. Then his mom told him that the wine was gone, implying that he should do something about it. Jesus ultimately did perform the miracle, but not before expressing a little affectionate annoyance to his mom: "Woman, why do you involve me? . . . My hour has not yet come" (John 2:4).

GRIEF

On more than one occasion, Jesus experienced grief. In his growing-up years, as we explored earlier, he probably grieved the loss of Joseph and some younger siblings or other relatives who died in infancy. We also have direct evidence in the Gospels that he mourned heavy losses. After his coworker and relative John the Baptist was murdered, we get a glimpse of Jesus grieving the loss: "John's disciples came and took his body and buried it. Then they went and told Jesus. When Jesus heard what had happened, he withdrew by boat privately to a solitary place" (Matthew 14:12–13). Other than the fact that Jesus withdrew to find solitude, we don't get much description of his grieving process.

We get more detail on how Jesus felt in the aftermath of his friend Lazarus's death. When Jesus arrived at Lazarus's house in Bethany, his sisters, Mary and Martha, were in the throes of grief. They asked Jesus why he didn't come sooner. They knew Jesus's power, and they knew he could have saved their brother. Jesus's response gives us a sense of how deeply he felt about losing Lazarus: "When Jesus saw [Mary] weeping, and the Jews who had come along with her also weeping, he was deeply moved in spirit and troubled" (John 11:33).

The Greek words John used express the deep emotional water Jesus was navigating. The word translated as "deeply moved" is *embrimaomai*, which was used to describe a horse snorting. Applied to humans, it describes a person barely containing their indignation.[1] It describes someone contending with deep emotions—sorrowful feelings that have an angry edge to them.[2] Jesus was sad, but it was an angry sadness. John also says Jesus was "troubled." The Greek word is *tarassō*, which describes being stirred up or experiencing inward disorder.[3] As a result of all these mixed-up feelings, "Jesus wept" (v. 35).

Two episodes of grief, two different responses. In one case, the death of John the Baptist, Jesus retreated and grieved in solitude. In the other case, the death of Lazarus, Jesus engaged with other mourners and felt a great deal of inner turmoil laced with anger. It's not the only time that Jesus felt that way.

ANGER

Anger might be the best known of the negative emotions Jesus felt. Most famously, Jesus cleared the temple of those who sought to corrupt and commercialize his Father's house. All four gospel writers tell of this incident, collectively describing Jesus angrily and publicly intervening in something he considered to be deeply wrong.[4] He objected to the money changers being present in the temple, and he protested the selling of animals. He felt that his Father's house was being transformed from a place of prayer into a marketplace—a den of robbers. And Jesus didn't just verbally proclaim what was wrong; he physically intervened. John tells us that Jesus made a whip of cords to drive the livestock out of the temple (2:15). He flipped over furniture. He flung the coins off the money changers' tables. Can you imagine the metal coins clattering on the stone ground when Jesus scattered their stacks of money? Mark explains that Jesus "would not allow anyone to carry merchandise through the temple courts" (11:16). In other words, he physically blocked their way. This would have caused quite a commotion, which is why, I imagine, this incident is recorded in all four gospels. Everyone remembered Jesus's anger on public display.

Now, just because Jesus physically intervened in the temple in this way does not give us permission to similarly act out on whatever anger we feel. Jesus was doing something related to his core mission and based on his unique authority as the

Son of God. Still, we have all felt righteous anger and can see ourselves in him, even in such an extraordinary moment.

At other times, Jesus used words to intervene when he saw flagrant wrongdoing. He famously lashed out at the Pharisees for their hypocrisy, arrogance, and legalism. In Matthew 23, Jesus publicly excoriated the Pharisees with indictments like, "Woe to you, teachers of the law and Pharisees, you hypocrites! You shut the door of the kingdom of heaven in people's faces. You yourselves do not enter, nor will you let those enter who are trying to" (v. 13). And, "Woe to you, teachers of the law and Pharisees, you hypocrites! You clean the outside of the cup and dish, but inside they are full of greed and self-indulgence. Blind Pharisee! First clean the inside of the cup and dish, and then the outside also will be clean" (vv. 25–26).

Jesus's anger over poor stewardship of leadership—or outright spiritual abuse—helps us to see that when we feel disturbed or angry about such behavior in our modern world, we are right to feel that way. Let's consider one more negative emotion that Jesus experienced.

DISTRESS

On the eve of Jesus's crucifixion, he experienced acute distress in the garden of Gethsemane. He was emotionally overwhelmed, as any human would be when facing certain, agonizing death. In that grim moment, Jesus said to some of his disciples, "My soul is overwhelmed with sorrow to the point of death. Stay here and keep watch with me" (Matthew 26:38). The Greek word translated as "soul" is *psychē* and refers to one's inner life.[5] Jesus's emotional life was underwater, flooded with sorrow to the point of death. In other words, he couldn't stand it. He was inundated with sadness and fear.

In a parallel description in Luke's gospel, we read that "being in anguish, he prayed more earnestly, and his sweat was like drops of blood falling to the ground" (22:44). The word "anguish" is a translation of the ancient Greek word *agōnia*, which sometimes described the dread athletes felt before an important competition.[6] Jesus was praying in anguish, dreading what was to come. It is no stretch to say that this was a mental health crisis, a moment of acute spiritual and psychological distress. Jesus experienced this, as we sometimes do too.

OUR EVERYDAY MOMENTS

Jesus felt the negative emotions we feel, like annoyance, grief, anger, and distress. And these feelings bothered him. As we highlighted in the introduction, one of the risks we run in considering Jesus's humanity is thinking that the difficulties he experienced weren't that hard for him because he's God. But that kind of thinking reveals that we don't really believe he was fully human in addition to being fully God. It's safe to say that, being fully human, when Jesus felt negative (but normal) human emotions, they were not pleasant experiences for him.

If you've experienced the unsettling mixture of feelings that combine into grief, Jesus understands. If you have felt sadness, distraction, hopelessness, rage, and bewilderment over a loss—if you have felt stirred up—Jesus felt that on more than one occasion. He created these feelings, he experienced them, and he knows all about what you've gone through.

If you have ever felt—or been made to feel—that it's a sign of weak faith to battle with negative feelings or struggle with your mental health, that's a lie. Remember that Jesus himself had moments when he felt emotionally overwhelmed, as did other key biblical figures.

Jonah told God, "I'm so angry I wish I were dead" (Jonah 4:9). Elijah said to God, "I have had enough, Lord. . . . Take my life; I am no better than my ancestors" (1 Kings 19:4). These were two of God's prophets coping with moments of real, human distress. If they experienced times when their mental health was cratering, we certainly will. We shouldn't feel shame about that. In *Letters to Malcolm*, C. S. Lewis explains it this way: "Some people feel guilty about their anxieties and regard them as a defect of faith. I don't agree at all. They are afflictions, not sins. Like all afflictions, they are, if we can so take them, our share in the Passion of Christ."[7]

Just before his arrest, Jesus told his disciples to not let their hearts be troubled (John 14:1). He did not dispense this advice lightly. Jesus knew what it meant to feel troubled, and he was encouraging his disciples to avoid falling into that sort of despair. Jesus knew well how it felt to have a heavy emotional life at times.

Centuries before Jesus's birth, when Isaiah had a vision of who the Messiah would be, he described him as a man of sorrow:

> He was despised and rejected by mankind,
> a man of suffering, and familiar with pain.
> Like one from whom people hide their faces
> he was despised, and we held him in low
> esteem.
>
> (Isaiah 53:3)

Jesus was familiar with pain. When you feel that pain is all too familiar or that sorrow marks your days, you can trust that Jesus truly understands the weight of those feelings. Emotions are part of our God-given design. We don't need to dismiss or minimize them. Most emotions are not inherently sinful, but without God's help in processing them they can easily become sinful or corrosive in their expression. This is why Paul warned the Ephesian Christians, "In your anger do not sin" (Ephesians 4:26).

We've covered just a few of the heavy emotions Jesus experienced. There are others, I'm sure. He certainly would have felt loneliness, fear, and frustration over the course of his childhood, adolescence, and adulthood. We can turn to him when we find ourselves tested in similar territory. If you're unsure how to talk to God about your feelings, try drawing a picture of the last year of your life. I was once led through an exercise like that, and I was surprised by how helpful it was. Draw or paint the picture, reflect on it, and then pray. Talk to God. Just describe what's on the page and ask Jesus to comfort you. He already knows how you feel, but he wants to hear it from you, just as any loving parent would want to hear their child express their feelings.

And we can be on the lookout for opportunities to remind others—brothers and sisters in Christ, and even those who don't yet believe in God—that Jesus knows about and understands their feelings. We can take our emotions to Jesus, knowing that he understands and resting in the fact that "he took up our pain and bore our suffering" (Isaiah 53:4).

QUESTIONS FOR GROUP DISCUSSION OR PERSONAL REFLECTION

- What surprised or challenged you about this chapter?
- Which feelings are hard to imagine Jesus experiencing? Why?
- What do we lose if we forget that Jesus had real feelings?
- How have you struggled to trust God when your emotional life is heavy?
- What is one step you can take this week to have a healthier, more biblical outlook on your emotions?

- If you could ask Jesus something about your emotional life and get an audible answer right now, what would you ask and why?

Jesus, it's jarring to think about you being annoyed, or grieving, or feeling angry, or experiencing mental anguish. But it's comforting to know you did, because sometimes I do too. Please help me to bear the burdens of this life, to not fall into persistent joylessness, to remember your ever-presence, and to recall your love that is evergreen. I recognize that there are aspects of my emotions and mental health that are beyond my control. Please help me to remember that I cannot keep perfect composure in my life, and that I need your help responding to my feelings that overwhelm me. If I need practical help from a doctor or counselor, help me to realize that and give me the courage to ask for help. I trust you and I trust in your love for me. Amen.

8

A Fractured Cultural Life

I've always gravitated toward old things: vintage instruments, dusty books, clacking typewriters, and creaking floors. Sometimes I can feel myself turning antique, especially when trying to explain to my kids what life was like growing up in the '90s.

Gobs of ink have been spilled about the personal and societal effects of social media, so forgive me as I spill a few drops more. First, social media has imported distant nations, cultures, and causes into our lives in real time. Our lives used to be affected mainly by those in close proximity to us: family members, neighbors, church congregations, classmates, coworkers, and community leaders. We would hear about national and international affairs intermittently on the news, and if we wanted to learn about far-off cultures, we could read about them in books. Now, we can find ourselves on the front lines of social and political happenings on the other side of the globe, and—if we choose to—we can stay in touch with everyone we have ever known.

This real-time global access means that our experiences are now more *and* less shared. There is ongoing, up-to-the-minute dialogue around key events in our country and our world. In that sense, our experiences seem more shared than they used to be. Dig a little deeper, however, and we realize that we have fewer truly shared cultural experiences. For example, a handful of TV networks and record labels used to curate pop culture for us. When a show or movie was popular, everyone watched it. When a song was a hit, everyone listened to it. Now there are dozens of networks and streaming platforms, thousands of shows and films available on demand, and countless musicians to discover. It has become exceedingly rare that we're all watching or listening to the same thing at the same time. Apart from unavoidable cultural milestones like the Super Bowl or the Olympics, our interests have splintered into a million fragments.

Another effect of social media is that we are more readily in touch with those who criticize us or who we might be inclined to debate. We have a greater awareness of Christians who think differently than we do, and we hear the amplified voices of those who hold different worldviews: people of other faiths and secular folks who sometimes disapprove of our biblical values.

So, our cultures are less homogeneous, we have fewer shared societal experiences, and we readily hear from our critics. All these effects, and others, add up to a much more fractured cultural experience than life before social media. I'll leave it to others to discern whether that fracturing has had a net positive or negative effect on our lives.

Jesus lived in a fractured culture too. We'll save first-century politics for the next chapter, but here we will explore the coming of Greco-Roman culture to Israel, outsiders' attitudes toward Jews, and Judean attitudes toward Galileans like Jesus.

PAGAN ATTITUDES TOWARD JEWS

Much changed for the people of Israel during the period between the Old and New Testaments. Most significantly, Alexander the Great and his Greek armies swept through the Mediterranean world and swallowed up everything in their path. After conquering more lands than anyone in history up to that point, Alexander established an empire that stretched from Greece all the way to present-day India. A raft of cultural changes followed in the wake of his armies, dramatically transforming the lives of those living in Alexander's dominion and that of his successors. Greek philosophy began to permeate the ancient Middle Eastern and Mediterranean world, as did Greek clothing, art, architecture, religion, iconography, and—perhaps most importantly—language. This is why the New Testament was originally written in Greek; it was the language spoken by most of the people in that part of the world at the time.

During Jesus's life, cities in and near Israel featured the touchstones of Greek culture, such as theaters, gymnasiums, public baths, Greek deities on altars and artwork, and coins with Greek inscriptions. Herod the Great was a renowned builder, as was his son Antipas. The cities and installations they built throughout Israel featured the latest of Greco-Roman technology and design.[1]

These cultural shifts were magnified and expanded when the Romans, who embraced and modified Greek culture, came to power. The Romans conquered many peoples in their rise to power during the decades before Jesus's life. Religiously speaking, most of these defeated nations were similar to the Romans: they were pagan polytheists. They were accustomed to the idea that certain nations and geographic locales were the dominions of particular gods or goddesses, and that powerful empires must have powerful deities behind them. In this respect, the Jewish people stood out. They were monotheists. They believed in their God, and even though they wove themselves into communities all over the Roman Empire, Jews rejected the worship of pagan gods and refused to ascribe divine attributes to Caesar as many of their neighbors did. Simply speaking, they were different. Larry Hurtado summarizes their distinctiveness:

> In the eyes of the ancient pagans, the Jews' refusal to worship any deity but their own, though often deemed bizarre and objectionable, was basically regarded as one, rather distinctive, example of national peculiarities. Whether resident in Roman Judaea or in their many diaspora locations, Jews were commonly thought of, and thought of themselves, as a distinct people. . . . Non-Jews, "pagans," seem to have found the Jewish refusal to honor their gods offensive, however, or at least annoying, and this must have contributed to the anti-Jewish sentiments expressed in a number of contemporary texts.[2]

Jews were viewed as overzealous in their religious devotion. Maybe you have felt something like that, like your Christian views are backward, over the top, or out of step with the age. The Jews of Jesus's day were seen this way by the dominant culture of the time, and it wasn't easy for them. In their homeland and in various communities spread around the Mediterranean, it was said, written, or implied that the Jews were peculiar and didn't fit in. Even so, Jesus purposefully engaged with people from the dominant culture who had prejudicial views toward his own people. He visited the vicinity of Tyre and commended the faith of a Canaanite woman (Matthew 15:21–28). He similarly applauded the faith of a Roman centurion (8:5–13) and offered teaching and healings in Gentile areas such as the Decapolis on the other side of the Sea of Galilee (Mark 5:1–20).

SAMARITAN ATTITUDES TOWARD JEWS

Closer to home, geographically speaking, were the Samaritans. They shared a religious and cultural heritage with the Jews, but there was hostility between the two peoples. The Samaritans saw themselves as the genuinely faithful remnant of early Israel, while the Jews viewed the Samaritans as outsiders who came into the land at a later date and adopted a partial and warped view of biblical faith.[3] The Samaritan territory cut a wide swath right through the heart of historic Israel, so Jews who were traveling between Galilee in the north and Judea in the south crossed the Jordan River and took the long way around to avoid going through Samaria and risking an altercation.[4] First-century historian Josephus records such an instance of violence:

> Now there arose a quarrel between the Samaritans and the Jews on the occasion following: It was the custom of the Galileans, when they came to [Jerusalem] at the festivals, to take their journeys through the country of the Samaritans; and at this time there lay, in the road they took, a village that was called Ginea, which was situated in the limits of Samaria and the great plain, where certain [locals] fought with the Galileans, and killed a great many of them.[5]

This tense relationship between Jews and Samaritans is on clear display in the gospel of John. Here we see Jesus deliberately go through Samaritan territory rather than take the safe way around to the east:

> So [Jesus] left Judea and went back once more to Galilee.

> Now he had to go through Samaria. So he came to a town in Samaria called Sychar, near the plot of ground Jacob had given to his son Joseph. Jacob's well was there, and Jesus, tired as he was from the journey, sat down by the well. It was about noon.
>
> When a Samaritan woman came to draw water, Jesus said to her, "Will you give me a drink?" (His disciples had gone into the town to buy food.)
>
> The Samaritan woman said to him, "You are a Jew and I am a Samaritan woman. How can you ask me for a drink?" (For Jews do not associate with Samaritans.) (4:3–9)

The division between Jews and Samaritans was another fault line in the fractured cultural experience of Jesus and his followers. Their beliefs were much more similar to each other than they were to Greco-Roman paganism, but they were different enough to cause persistent animosity.

There was a much greater gulf between first-century Jews and Samaritans than between Christian denominations today, but this kind of frustration is familiar to many of us. We have all felt similar fissures in our church experiences over matters of scriptural interpretation and historical tradition. We have witnessed or been a part of church splits. We have participated in or observed rancorous online debates, with diatribes launched as artillery toward brothers and sisters in Christ. We have watched as denominations are torn apart, with cavalier declarations by both sides of who is more original, more faithful, more biblical, more Christlike, more aligned with their founders' values. This kind of pain is hard to heal from, and Jesus must have experienced some of this in his interactions with Samaritans.

Jews like Jesus experienced cultural fractures with the onset of Greco-Roman hegemony, and they also experienced it with the Samaritans, their near neighbors. In the Roman Empire, Jews and Samaritans were religious minorities. But *Galilean* Jews like Jesus also experienced internal rifts between them and their Jewish relatives to the south in Judea.

JUDEAN ATTITUDES TOWARD GALILEANS

From what we can tell, many Judean Jews, who lived in the south of Israel near Jerusalem, viewed Galilean Jews as rustic, restless, unsophisticated, and sometimes rebellious.[6]

This perspective is evident in one episode recorded in the book of Acts. As the early church was establishing itself after Jesus's death and resurrection, Peter and some of the other Christian leaders were arrested and questioned by the Jewish ruling council, the Sanhedrin. Gamaliel, a respected member of that body, cautioned his fellow council members about overreacting to the activities of the earliest Christians. In his short speech, he alludes to a previous rebellion that originated in Galilee and came to nothing:

> Men of Israel, consider carefully what you intend to do to these men. Some time ago Theudas appeared, claiming to be somebody, and about four hundred men rallied to him. He was killed, all his followers were dispersed, and it all came to nothing. After him, Judas the Galilean appeared in the days of the census and led a band of people in revolt. He too was killed, and all his followers were scattered. Therefore, in the present case I advise you: Leave these men alone! Let them go! For if their purpose or activity is of human origin, it will fail. But if it is from God, you will not be able to stop these men;

> you will only find yourselves fighting against God. (Acts 5:35–39)

In addition to their reputation for rebellion, Galileans were viewed as less sophisticated than Jews from Judea, where the centers of Jewish religious authority were based. On one occasion, Nicodemus, a member of the Jewish religious elite, defended Jesus against what he considered to be hasty attacks on his character. His moderate view of Jesus was met with vitriol and condescending rhetoric toward Galileans: "Nicodemus, who had gone to Jesus earlier and who was one of their own number, asked, 'Does our law condemn a man without first hearing him to find out what he has been doing?' [The Pharisees] replied, 'Are you from Galilee, too? Look into it, and you will find that a prophet does not come out of Galilee'" (John 7:50–52).

Galileans were easily identified by their regional accent, which assisted Judean prejudice against them. For example, when Peter denied associating with Jesus, those standing nearby said, "Surely you are one of them, for you are a Galilean" (Mark 14:70), and "Surely you are one of them; your accent gives you away" (Matthew 26:73). In the Babylonian Talmud, Galilean accents were openly mocked.[7] Even though Jesus and his disciples shared much in common with their fellow Jews to the south, Galileans were out of their element in Jerusalem and Judea.[8]

The sometimes snobbish and superior attitude of Judeans toward Galileans is not unfamiliar to us. We detect the same condescension from urban Christians toward rural Christians, megachurch leaders toward pastors of small congregations, the educated toward the uneducated, seasoned Christians toward new believers, Western Christians toward non-Western Christians, and younger generations toward older generations (or the other way around). If you have ever felt yourself on the wrong side of condescension, split off from some segment of your community of faith, Jesus experienced the same things.

OUR EVERYDAY MOMENTS

If you, in the twenty-first century, have a sense of living in an ever-changing global marketplace of ideas, that is not unlike what Jews in Jesus's day experienced. Jesus lived in an era that was full of new ideas, technologies, styles, and philosophies—many imported from far-off places that were foreign to Israel. Jesus understands how it feels to sense the cultural foundations shifting under your feet.

Maybe you have felt this way. I know I have. As our world changes and new cultural contexts make their way to us via the internet and social media, we can feel like outsiders in our own lives, visitors in our own communities, strangers even in our families. The Jews were experiencing seismic cultural tremors with the influx of Greco-Roman culture, and Jesus felt the effects of that. He lived in a fractured and fracturing culture. He understands us when we feel disoriented by cultural changes and the splintering of things that once felt cohesive.

As we've seen, pagan residents of the empire viewed Jews with derision. Samaritans viewed Jews as adversaries. Judeans viewed Galileans as inferior. Jesus, as a Galilean Jew, was on the wrong side of all these relationships. He undoubtedly experienced ongoing tension in the background and moments of condescension and outright hostility.

In our own culturally fractured time, where there's little consensus and it feels like there are always antagonists at the ready, you can ask Jesus for calm and for comfort. You can ask the Spirit to give you an unfractured heart and to remind you that Jesus purposely engaged with Greeks, Romans, Samaritans, and Judeans—all those who looked down on people like him. He was for them even when they weren't for him, just like he was for us even when we were still God's enemies (Romans 5:10).

You can also ask Jesus to help you identify those people and groups that you may look down on. If we're honest with ourselves, we all have them. It could be someone with a different political perspective or a group that holds a different theological view than you're accustomed to. Perhaps you have negative knee-jerk views toward people from certain countries or who hail from a different region of your own country. Maybe you find yourself easily irked by people who behave differently than you do online or who have seemingly unhelpful perspectives on parenting or a misguided work ethic.

There are all sorts of ways that we can find ourselves thinking we're superior to others. Jesus, the one who is actually and rightfully superior, can help you recognize those corners of your heart that are darkened by prejudice. He knows how it felt to be treated prejudicially, and he wants to free you from the instinct to treat others that way.

And if he does begin to change you in this area, you may find yourself—like he did—building bridges to whoever the Samaritans and centurions are in your life. When that happens, there may be some people in your life who don't understand what you're doing or even criticize you for it. They would prefer to leave the cultural chasms unbridged. If people are irritated by your efforts to be a bridge-building ambassador in the name of Jesus, it means that you're doing something right.

QUESTIONS FOR GROUP DISCUSSION OR PERSONAL REFLECTION

- What surprised or challenged you about this chapter?
- What new cultural influences have come into your life in the past decade? How have they affected you?

- Is there a group of people who look down on you? How do they make you feel, and how can you follow Jesus's example in responding to them?
- What is one step you can take this week to build a bridge toward someone on the other side of a cultural divide?
- If you could ask Jesus something about your cultural life and get an audible answer right now, what would you ask and why?

Try praying Psalm 13 as if they're your own words. Let the emotional realism and spiritual truth comfort you as you seek an unfractured heart in the midst of fractured times.

How long, LORD? Will you forget me forever?
  How long will you hide your face from me?
How long must I wrestle with my thoughts
  and day after day have sorrow in my heart?
  How long will my enemy triumph over me?

Look on me and answer, LORD my God.
  Give light to my eyes, or I will sleep in death,
and my enemy will say, "I have overcome him,"
  and my foes will rejoice when I fall.

But I trust in your unfailing love;
  my heart rejoices in your salvation.
I will sing the LORD's praise,
  for he has been good to me.

9

A Troubling Political Life

Our political perspectives, however sensible they seem to us, tend to become bothersome to other people once they exit our minds through our mouths or by our ever-posting fingertips. This is why politics used to be a subject carefully avoided with friends and family members: it inevitably leads to conflict. Now, because of social media and a never-sleeping news cycle, the subject is out in the open, and nearly everything has become politicized. On the one hand, we lament this reality and want to stay out of it. But on the other, we easily find ourselves continually contributing to it, sometimes in unhelpful ways.

Even before the advent of twenty-first-century technologies, representative democracy was somewhat irritating. It is inefficient by design so that one person or party cannot clutch perpetually onto power. Here in America, we have overlapping layers of power: federal, state, county, and city governments. There are two main political parties and a host of smaller factions and independent political leaders. There are other local representative bodies, like school boards, that wield considerable influence. Citizens are invited to share their perspectives, become involved in the process, and peacefully protest when something seems wrong. With elections unfolding regularly, power is constantly shifting in our society, and there are endless disagreements about how our government should function and what our society should be like. Even in a relatively healthy democracy, politics can be frustrating.

Jesus and his contemporaries had political lives too. Of course, their political landscape was considerably different from a twenty-first-century Western democracy, but they too felt like political topics were inescapable. Not because of the internet, but because their country was occupied and Roman propaganda was everywhere. Jesus and his family would have understood the routine irritations, abuses of power, ethical compromises, and ugly machinations that come with an occupying imperial force and the local rulers who cooperated with them. Citizens who toil today under the thumb of authoritarian regimes have a better sense of how Jesus and his family must have felt. We who live in democracies can only understand so much, but it's good for us to try.

In the gospel of Luke, we get a bird's-eye view of the overlapping political powers at work in first-century Judea: "In the fifteenth year of the reign of Tiberius Caesar—when Pontius Pilate was governor of Judea, Herod tetrarch of Galilee, his brother Philip tetrarch of Iturea and Traconitis, and Lysanias tetrarch of Abilene—during the high-priesthood of Annas and Caiaphas, the word of God came to John son of Zechariah in the wilderness" (3:1–2).

Luke, the consummate historian, covered a lot of ground in these two verses. His aim was to put a precise date on the beginning of John the Baptist's ministry. The way to do that was to describe all the key people in power at the time. He mentions Tiberius Caesar, the Roman emperor, and his underling

Pontius Pilate, the governor of the Roman province of Judea. He lists three tetrarchs, local pseudo-kings ruling in cooperation with Rome: Herod Antipas, Philip, and Lysanias. Luke also mentions two Jewish high priests—Annas and Caiaphas. They held spiritual leadership roles that had become highly politicized after Rome's rule began in Judea.

Let's consider the political landscape that Jesus's family had to contend with as they went about their mostly ordinary lives in Galilee.

THE ROMANS

The historic homeland of Israel officially became a province of the Roman Empire when Jesus was about ten years old, though Roman power had been established in the area decades earlier. This was not the Jews' first experience with imperial occupation. Their ancestors had been absorbed into and ruled in succession by the Assyrians, Babylonians, Persians, and then the Greeks after Alexander's conquests. During Jesus's lifetime, the Roman province of Judea was governed by a mid-level Roman administrator called a prefect.[1] This is the position that Pontius Pilate held, his main goals being to keep the peace and promote the priorities of Rome.[2]

Pilate served in this position from AD 26–36, which means that at Jesus's trial, he was toward the end of his tenure as prefect of Judea. Prior to Jesus's trial, Pilate seems to have gotten himself into trouble with his superiors for deliberately antagonizing the Jews—sometimes violently.[3] First-century historian Josephus recorded several instances of Pilate's brutal tendencies. On one occasion, Pilate attempted to construct an aqueduct in Jerusalem using money taken from the temple's coffers, which of course offended the Jews. When they gathered in large numbers to protest, Pilate ordered undercover soldiers into the crowd, and on his signal they unsheathed their blades and killed a great number of Jewish protesters.[4] There is also a cryptic reference to Pilate's violence in the gospel of Luke: "There were some present at that time who told Jesus about the Galileans whose blood Pilate had mixed with their sacrifices" (13:1).

Pilate was the representative of Roman power in Judea, and he was no force for good. Rome, the far-off capital of the most powerful government in the world, was mostly unmoved by the grievances of those who lived in distant provinces. Jesus lived out his days under this regime. He was challenged about his perspective on paying taxes to Caesar, and in the end found himself in chains standing before a Roman official who wielded the power of capital punishment.

THE HIGH PRIEST

Underneath and alongside Rome's imperial power was the power of the high priest in Jerusalem. The high priest had long played an important spiritual and administrative role within Israel, a position that was tested and redefined once Rome asserted itself in Judea.[5] The Romans knew the Jews were highly sensitive about their religion and temple operations, so they allowed the Jewish leadership some latitude to manage their internal affairs. But the role of high priest became politicized because Rome demanded that the high priests be deferential to Caesar. Consider Pontius Pilate's predecessor, Valerius Gratus. He was the Roman prefect of Judea from AD 15 to 26. During his tenure, Gratus fired four high priests and installed their replacements.[6] The prefects expected the Jewish religious leadership to be loyal to Rome—and at times the Jewish leaders threatened to report the prefect to Rome if he was stepping out of line. This uncomfortable dynamic was on display during Jesus's trial, when the Jewish leaders brought Jesus to Pontius Pilate. They told him, "If you let this man go, you are no friend of Caesar. Anyone who claims to be a king opposes Caesar" (John 19:12). They were suggesting to Pilate that regarding Jesus, they were perhaps more loyal to Rome than he was.

At the time of Jesus's ministry, Caiaphas was the high priest (Matthew 26:3; John 11:49). But his father-in-law Annas was a former high priest and continued to wield power behind the scenes as the head of the family.[7] The Gospels capture this state of affairs: Caiaphas and Annas sharing—to some extent—the high priestly power. Luke described John the Baptist's ministry beginning "during the high-priesthood of Annas and Caiaphas" (Luke 3:2). In his narration of Jesus's arrest and trial, John described Jesus being questioned by Annas and then Caiaphas, who are both referred to as the high priest:

> Then the detachment of soldiers with its commander and the Jewish officials arrested Jesus. They bound him and brought him first to Annas, who was the father-in-law of Caiaphas, the high priest that year. . . .
>
> Meanwhile, the high priest questioned Jesus about his disciples and his teaching.
>
> "I have spoken openly to the world," Jesus replied. "I always taught in synagogues or at the temple, where all the Jews come together. I said nothing in secret. Why question me? Ask those who heard me. Surely they know what I said."
>
> When Jesus said this, one of the officials nearby slapped him in the face. "Is this the way you answer the high priest?" he demanded.
>
> "If I said something wrong," Jesus replied, "testify as to what is wrong. But if I spoke the truth, why did you strike me?" Then Annas sent him bound to Caiaphas the high priest. (18:12–13, 19–24)

The high priest was called to be a spiritual and community leader, bringing glory to the Lord through his shepherding of God's people and wise stewardship of the temple operations. Sadly, politics polluted that role. In defense of the high priests in this era, they had little choice; the Romans brutally imposed their will on the Jews, and Jewish leadership was forced to cope with that reality. In the case of Annas and Caiaphas, however, it appears their family was all too eager to play the game and mingle political and spiritual power. In Jesus's interaction with the high priest, he simply asked why he was being questioned. But in such a corrupt and politically charged environment, questioning the high priest in any way was considered offensive.

HEROD ANTIPAS

There is more than one Herod in the New Testament. The two best known are Herod the Great and his son Herod Antipas. Herod the Great ruled over the Jews on behalf of Rome during Jesus's infancy, notoriously trying to track down and kill the newborn Jesus after the Magi's visit. This is the Herod of our Christmas stories. After his death, his kingdom was divided between his sons. One of his sons, Herod Antipas, was given the part of his father's kingdom that included Galilee, where Jesus grew up and carried out most of his public ministry. Antipas is the Herod of our Good Friday and Easter stories. He is also the one, as we learned in chapter 2, who built Sepphoris.

In Luke 3, Luke describes Herod Antipas as "tetrarch of Galilee" (v. 1). The title "tetrarch" meant "ruler of a fourth," which has to do with Herod Antipas ruling a portion of his father's old kingdom. Tetrarch was a lower title than king, but Caesar permitted Antipas to continue using the name Herod as a title that carried informal king-like connotations.[8]

Unsurprisingly, Herod Antipas was a negative factor in

Jesus's life and ministry. Antipas murdered John the Baptist, Jesus's friend and relative (Matthew 14:1–12; Mark 6:14–29; Luke 9:7–9). Jesus spoke about Antipas, telling his disciples, "Watch out for the yeast of the Pharisees and that of Herod" (Mark 8:15). On another occasion, "some Pharisees came to Jesus and said to him, 'Leave this place and go somewhere else. Herod wants to kill you.' He replied, 'Go tell that fox, "I will keep on driving out demons and healing people today and tomorrow, and on the third day I will reach my goal"'" (Luke 13:31–32).

It seems that Jesus never directly interacted with Herod Antipas until his trial, and when they were finally in the same room, Jesus refused to speak. "When [Pilate] learned that Jesus was under Herod's jurisdiction, he sent him to Herod, who was also in Jerusalem at that time. When Herod saw Jesus, he was greatly pleased, because for a long time he had been wanting to see him. From what he had heard about him, he hoped to see him perform a sign of some sort. He plied him with many questions, but Jesus gave him no answer" (23:7–9).

The overlapping powers of Jesus's day often disagreed with each other, adding another layer of uncertainty and stress for the citizenry. The discord between the high priests and Pilate was famously on display during Jesus's trial. There was also tension between Pilate and Herod Antipas. In one instance, Pilate murdered some Galileans, citizens of Antipas's domain (Luke 13:1). Antipas had written a letter to Caesar explaining how Pilate went out of his way to make trouble for the Jewish people, a clear violation of his mandate as a Roman peacekeeper.[9] It was Jesus's trial, in fact, that allowed these two regional rulers to mend fences. After Pilate sent Jesus to Herod, Herod returned the favor in an act of deference to the Roman prefect: "Then Herod and his soldiers ridiculed and mocked [Jesus]. Dressing him in an elegant robe, they sent him back to Pilate. That day Herod and Pilate became friends—before this they had been enemies" (23:11–12).

OUR EVERYDAY MOMENTS

We now see the political complexity for those who lived where and when Jesus did. Imperial power radiated from far-off Rome, represented locally by the Roman prefect (Pontius Pilate). Spiritual and cultural power emitted from Jerusalem under the leadership of the high priest (Annas and Caiaphas). Intersecting these two spheres were Jewish pseudo-kings like Herod Antipas who wielded regional political power. None of these powers were democratically elected.

Maybe you've felt like the national leaders of your country are far away and mostly uninterested in the struggles of your community. On the other hand, you may feel that they intrude into your life in unwelcome or disrespectful ways. The Jews of Jesus's day knew exactly how that felt. If you feel powerless to affect the culture and policies of your nation's capital, Jesus and his peers probably felt similarly about Rome.

Have you ever interacted with local officials whom you felt should be on your side, but they seemed enamored instead with their power over you? Those situations can be deeply frustrating, and Jesus and his peers had similar experiences. Or maybe you've felt caught between two layers of government that are not on the same page. Perhaps the values of your national government do not align with those of your local government. Maybe the leaders of your child's school do not see the world the same way as the governor of your state does. Maybe city and county officials are arguing about some aspect of your neighborhood's development or about the response to a local crisis. Have you ever felt the powerlessness of being caught in the middle of competing political forces?

Jesus certainly did, and you can turn to him to express your frustration and seek peace and wisdom on whether to become more—or less—engaged with politics.

In terms of spiritual leadership, maybe you have felt that certain Christian groups or leaders have become too entangled with politics or too cozy with specific politicians or governmental initiatives. Or maybe the power in your church or denomination seems to be concentrated in the hands of too few people, or there are pastoral dynasties in place that make little room for new leaders. These challenges of spiritual leadership were a common reality for first-century Jews.

Jesus's life unfolded under the authority of flawed and often corrupt human governments. This is yet another way that he was tested, just as we are, so we can confidently approach him and ask for wisdom, patience, courage, and a Christlike perspective on citizenship.

QUESTIONS FOR GROUP DISCUSSION OR PERSONAL REFLECTION

- What surprised or challenged you about this chapter?
- In what ways does the political landscape of Jesus's day remind you of our modern world?
- How would you describe your feelings about politics? What are the greatest sources of frustration for you?
- Do you feel you should become more or less politically engaged? Why?
- What is one step you can take this week to have a healthier relationship with politics?
- If you could ask Jesus something about your political life and get an audible answer right now, what would you ask and why?

Lord Jesus, I need your help to think rightly about government and politics. I sometimes feel overwhelmed by the constant torrent of information and by the ugly disagreements between politicians and different spheres of government. It brings me comfort to know that you had to wade through life with overlapping levels of political power. Thank you for being willing to come to earth to rescue me, and to live with such frustrating realities like human politics. Holy Spirit, remind me that you are the king of my life and of the world. Help me to rest in that and to be a wise, Christlike, responsible citizen. Amen.

10

A Tangled Social Life

"It is not good for the man to be alone." These are some of the first words God ever said about a human being, recorded in Genesis 2:18. In his eternal three-in-oneness, God is inherently social, and we were made to resemble him in this way. Whether we consider ourselves introverts or extroverts, social butterflies or happy recluses, we are all social creatures with a collection of new and old relationships that ebb and flow over the course of our lives. Some relationships are closer than others, some last longer than others, some are quite mutual, others struggle for reciprocity. Our relationships have the potential to be wellsprings of joy in our lives, but they can also become bogs of pain.

I suspect that our lives would be easier if all our relationships could fit into tidy, predictable categories. If our bosses could just be bosses, our coworkers could just be coworkers, our friends could just be friends, our neighbors could just be neighbors, and so on. But what happens when our social lives feel tangled up, as they often do? What happens when you develop a friendship with a supervisor? Or start dating a coworker? Or a neighbor shares leadership responsibilities with you on a school committee? Or a friend becomes a creative collaborator? When the lines blur in our relationships, it can become challenging.

Anyone in leadership has experienced this. It's challenging to be someone's pastor while simultaneously serving as their boss on a church staff. It's difficult to serve as a church elder and interact as equals with fellow congregants. Teachers, police officers, and other public servants have similar experiences. Building or maintaining friendships with peers can be complicated when you have some form of authority or leadership responsibility. Parents can't simply be parents; what it means to be a parent evolves over the years. Many struggle to move from the authoritative position required during their kids' younger years to something more like an adviser as their children grow into adults.

Jesus had a social life too. Just like us, he had nested layers of relationships, and the boundaries between them were somewhat fuzzy. He had an inner circle, disciples, personal friends, a best friend, acquaintances, and of course thousands of people who felt like they knew him personally but in fact did not. Let's consider the jumble of social relationships in Jesus's life and find some of our experiences in his.

HIS INNER CIRCLE

When Jesus began his public ministry, he chose twelve disciples to form an inner circle. They would spend time with him, share leadership responsibilities, and—most importantly—learn from him so they could be faithful bearers of his message and mission once he ascended into heaven. But within the twelve disciples, he had an even closer inner circle of three: Peter and two friends of his, the sons of Zebedee, James and John. Jesus encountered the trio when they were going about their daily work as fishermen on the Sea of Galilee. Luke records their reaction after Jesus performed a miracle and caused them to catch a stunningly large number of fish: "[Peter] and all his companions were astonished at the catch of fish they had taken, and so were James and John, the sons of Zebedee, Simon's partners" (Luke 5:9–10).

As Jesus went about his ministry, he was careful not to reveal too much of his identity too quickly. He didn't want to arouse the attention of the authorities too early so he could have enough time to share his message with as many people as possible. Even among his disciples, there were certain experiences that he reserved only for Peter, James, and John.

On one occasion he raised a twelve-year-old girl to life. Jesus was already performing healings and miracles, but this one was of a higher order, foreshadowing his own resurrection. Later, when Jesus raised his friend Lazarus from the dead, the authorities resolved to take his life because they knew that if he continued to perform resurrections, then everyone would believe in him. So, when Jesus raised the young girl to life at an earlier stage of his ministry, he wanted to limit the number of people who witnessed such an unmistakably divine intervention. Mark describes the scene: "While Jesus was still speaking, some people came from the house of Jairus, the synagogue leader. 'Your daughter is dead,' they said. 'Why bother the teacher anymore?' Overhearing what they said, Jesus told him, 'Don't be afraid; just believe.' He did not let anyone follow him except Peter, James and John the brother of James" (5:35–37).

Having limited his disciples to three, Jesus further limited the witnesses to the little girl's parents: "After he put them all out, he took the child's father and mother and the disciples who were with him, and went in where the child was. He took her by the hand and said to her, '*Talitha koum!*' (which means 'Little girl, I say to you, get up!'). Immediately the girl stood up and began to walk around (she was twelve years old). At this they were completely astonished. He gave strict orders not to let anyone know about this, and told them to give her something to eat" (vv. 40–43).

Peter and the brothers were invited into another experience that helped them realize Jesus's true identity, and once again they were instructed to keep it to themselves until the appropriate time.

> After six days Jesus took with him Peter, James and John the brother of James, and led them up a high mountain by themselves. There he was transfigured before them. His face shone like the sun, and his clothes became as white as the light. . . .
>
> A bright cloud covered them, and a voice from the cloud said, "This is my Son, whom I love; with him I am well pleased. Listen to him!"
>
> When the disciples heard this, they fell facedown to the ground, terrified. But Jesus came and touched them. "Get up," he said. "Don't be afraid." When they looked up, they saw no one except Jesus.
>
> As they were coming down the mountain, Jesus instructed them, "Don't tell anyone what you have seen, until the Son of Man has been raised from the dead." (Matthew 17:1–2, 5–9)

Jesus trusted these three men with the full knowledge of his divine identity earlier than most of his followers, who instead came to a more gradual realization. He also trusted Peter, James, and John on a personal level, asking them to be present with him during his darkest hour: "Then Jesus went with his disciples to a place called Gethsemane, and he said to them, 'Sit here while I go over there and pray.' He took Peter and the two sons of Zebedee along with him, and he began to be sorrowful and troubled" (26:36–37).

I wonder what it must have been like for Peter, James, and John. I'm sure they felt special, being treated with such trust by their Lord. They may have also wondered why he chose them for the privilege of these experiences. It seems their special access to Jesus caused some pride and even competition among them. We see glimpses of this in the Gospels: John and Peter have a literal footrace to get to the empty tomb (John 20:4), and James and John ask to be the top two people in Jesus's kingdom (Mark 10:37).

Within this innermost circle, John seems to have been Jesus's best friend. Years later, he went on to write the gospel of John, in which he referred to himself as "the disciple whom Jesus loved." This disciple was especially close to Jesus during the Last Supper: "Jesus was troubled in spirit and testified, 'Very truly I tell you, one of you is going to betray me.' His disciples stared at one another, at a loss to know which of them he meant. One of them, the disciple whom Jesus loved, was reclining next to him" (13:21–23).

Not long after, when most of Jesus's friends and followers had abandoned him, John is there at the foot of the cross. In that dark moment, Jesus entrusted the future care of his mother to his best friend: "Near the cross of Jesus stood his mother, his mother's sister, Mary the wife of Clopas, and Mary Magdalene. When Jesus saw his mother there, and the disciple whom he loved standing nearby, he said to her, 'Woman, here is your son,' and to the disciple, 'Here is your mother.' From that time on, this disciple took her into his home" (19:25–27). As the eldest son in his family, Jesus had been looking after his widowed mother for some time. It makes sense that he would entrust her care to John, who seems to have been his closest friend.

HIS FRIENDS

Beyond Jesus's inner circle, there was another group of people who were his friends who also happened to be his followers. The other nine disciples seem to have fallen into this category. They weren't exactly peers, and Jesus was less open with them than he was with Peter, James, and John. Still, in some of his final words to the disciples before his arrest, Jesus called them friends: "Greater love has no one than this: to lay down one's life for one's friends. You are my friends if you do what I command. I no longer call you servants, because a servant does not know his master's business. Instead, I have called you friends, for everything that I learned from my Father I have made known to you" (John 15:13–15).

But Jesus also had friends outside of his twelve disciples. He had family friends who probably reached back to his growing-up years in Nazareth. Jesus and his mother were invited to a wedding, which implies that these were mutual family friends. Also, when Jesus went missing in Jerusalem as a twelve-year-old boy, his parents frantically searched for him: "Thinking he was in their company, they traveled on for a day. Then they began looking for him among their relatives and friends" (Luke 2:44). Mary and Joseph had friends, and they apparently traveled with them to Jerusalem for certain holidays. Jesus would have known these people as friends for most of his life.

When I was growing up in Texas, our extended family lived on both coasts: some in Northern California, the rest in New England. We became close friends with another family who also had no relatives in the Lone Star State, so we would spend holidays together. I have one brother, and this family also had two boys our ages, so we had a lot in common. It became a tradition for our two families to spend Christmas Eve together. We would go out to dinner for Tex-Mex and then go together to the Christmas Eve service at our church. Then we would stay up late playing games at one of our houses. These are some of my happiest memories from my youth. I'm sure you have similar stories to tell about family and friends, and so did Jesus.

Jesus also had close friends who were partners in his ministry, people like Mary Magdalene, Joanna, and Susanna: "After this, Jesus traveled about from one town and village to another, proclaiming the good news of the kingdom of God. The Twelve were with him, and also some women who had been cured of evil spirits and diseases: Mary (called Magdalene) from whom seven demons had come out; Joanna the wife of Chuza, the manager of Herod's household; Susanna; and many others. These women were helping to support them out of their own means" (Luke 8:1–3). It's reasonable to assume they were close, but their friendship may have been more like a working friendship. They were in the trenches together.

Mary Magdalene may have been the closest to Jesus out of this group. She had the courage to be present during those agonizing hours that Jesus hung from the cross, she saw where he was buried, and she was entrusted by Jesus with being one of the first to witness his resurrection. In fact, Mary seems to have been the first person that the risen Christ conversed with. He revealed his identity to his friend by simply speaking her name, "Mary" (John 20:16).

Jesus also seems to have been especially close to the family of Mary, Martha, and Lazarus, who lived in Bethany. "As Jesus and his disciples were on their way, he came to a village where a woman named Martha opened her home to him. She had a sister called Mary, who sat at the Lord's feet listening to what he said" (Luke 10:38–39). Martha, apparently stressed out by the responsibilities of hosting Jesus and the other guests, blurted out, "Lord, don't you care that my sister has left me to do the work by myself? Tell her to help me!" (v. 40). Imagine being comfortable enough with Jesus to say something like that! To have that kind of confidence, Martha really must have been his friend. Jesus replied with the compassion we would expect from Martha's good friend, who also happened to be the Lord: "Martha, Martha, . . . you are worried and upset about many things" (v. 41). Then he gently encouraged her to follow Mary's example and prioritize spending time with him.

Later, when Lazarus became sick and died, the sisters asked for Jesus's help, describing their brother as beloved by Jesus: "Now a man named Lazarus was sick. He was from Bethany, the village of Mary and her sister Martha. (This Mary, whose brother Lazarus now lay sick, was the same one who poured perfume on the Lord and wiped his feet with her hair.) So the sisters sent word to Jesus, 'Lord, the one you love is sick'" (John 11:1–3).

When Lazarus died without Jesus's help, both sisters put Jesus on the spot with words that could only come from a trusted friend: "If you had been here, my brother would not have died" (John 11:21, 32). Jesus responded by doing what a true friend would do. He asked where Lazarus was buried, and then he went there and cried with Mary and Martha (vv. 34–35).

THE CROWDS

Throngs of people followed Jesus because of his life-changing teachings and because of the spectacle of his miracles. Many people in first-century Galilee were poor and struggling, so the prospect of a miraculous intervention into their life was thrilling. Luke describes the crowds almost crushing Jesus, and how they were always trying to find him (Luke 8:42). These were people who felt like they knew Jesus, or wanted to know him, and they expected help from him. Of course, Jesus knew them because of his divine knowledge, but he didn't know them on a personal, human level. In a sense, the crowds had with Jesus something like a parasocial relationship, in which someone feels a strong affection for or attachment to a public figure as if they know each other.

However we might describe his relationship with the large crowds that followed him around, one thing is clear: Jesus loved and cared for them all. "When he saw the crowds, he had compassion on them, because they were harassed and helpless, like sheep without a shepherd" (Matthew 9:36).

OUR EVERYDAY MOMENTS

The circumstances of Jesus's ministry and his relationships with his disciples were extraordinary, of course, but we can relate to certain elements of Jesus's tangled social life. Jesus had a best friend, an inner circle, a varied group of old and new friends, and people who thought of him as a friend who actually did not know him well. We all have such layers in our social world, and people do not fall into neat categories.

Do you have a best friend, or an inner circle of friends whom you trust with your deepest feelings and secret struggles? Jesus had people like that in his life, and he wants you to have those kinds of friendships too. If you have them, thank God for such a wonderful gift! If you wish you had them, ask God to help you make friends. In some seasons of life, friendships come easily. At others, you may need to take proactive steps to cultivate new or deepening friendships. Jesus knows how it feels to make friends, and he'll help you.

Have you ever experienced tensions between some of your friends? Have you felt one of them angling for a closer relationship with you or expressing frustration about being left out of something? Kids experience this with birthday parties, neighborhood friendships, and sports teams, but we continue to have similar moments as we age: Who should we invite to our birthday celebration? Who should be in our bridal party? Which friends should we take a vacation with? Who do we sit with at church? Which of our kids' friendships should we prioritize? When something painful happens in our lives, who should we confide in? How will our other friends feel when they later discover they were among the last to hear our news?

Maybe there is tension right now between two of your friends, and they came to mind as you read the last few sentences. Or perhaps you unintentionally made someone feel left out and you feel badly about it. Steering through these knotted social dynamics can be challenging, and Jesus must have experienced something similar. Ask him to help you know how to repair that situation.

Have you had to comfort a frustrated or grieving friend? Have you ever had friends whom you disappointed, or who disappointed you? Maybe a friend of yours hoped you would use your position, resources, or influence to help them, and you couldn't or wouldn't. Have you ever felt like there are strings attached in some of your friendships, or that people are putting expectations on you that you may not be able to fulfill? Jesus certainly had to contend with those dynamics.

Has someone interacted with you as if you know each other, possibly because of your reputation, your position, or your online presence? You may not know much about them, but they seem to know all about you. Or maybe they're an acquaintance who is more invested in building a friendship than you are. It can be challenging to navigate those uneven relationships. Again, ask Jesus to show you what steps to take to make the relationship more reciprocal, or perhaps to gracefully clarify for the other person that you don't have the time or energy to invest further.

Jesus would have experienced the ups and downs of his social life, just as we do. There would have been seasons of plenty with lots of family and like-minded friends around, and undoubtedly his close friendships were a joyful and life-giving part of his human experiences. On the other hand, there would have been times of frustration or loneliness. Our social lives are rarely exactly as we would like, and Jesus experienced this too. We need God's wisdom in navigating the churn of relationships in our lives, and he is able to give us the wise lenses we need.

QUESTIONS FOR GROUP DISCUSSION OR PERSONAL REFLECTION

- What surprised or challenged you about this chapter?
- In what ways do you see yourself in Jesus's web of social relationships?
- How might you follow Jesus's approach to his social life?
- What do you think is the value of having a trusted inner circle, and how can you navigate the feelings of other friends who are not in that circle but who might want to be?
- Have you ever felt left out of someone else's inner circle? How can you trust God with your feelings about that?
- What is one step you can take this week to infuse wisdom into your social life?
- If you could ask Jesus something about your social life and get an audible answer right now, what would you ask and why?

Lord Jesus, help me to think wisely about my social life, which often feels tangled up. It's comforting to know that you had overlapping layers of friends, and that you understand the joys and hurts that come with letting people into my life. Help me to be kind to those friends whom I must keep at arm's length and to process my disappointment in other friends who I feel have let me down. Help me to feel your presence when I feel lonely. I'm so glad to know that you know me best and are always with me. You won't let me down. Help me to rest in that. Amen.

11

A Routine Spiritual Life

Going through the motions gets a bad rap. In the modern Western Protestant world, feelings are on the throne of our spiritual lives. This is especially true in the evangelical branch of Western Protestantism. For many, our emotional experiences of spirituality are the main indicator of whether our faith is real and growing. If we don't experience a great swell of emotion during our conversion, or prayer, or baptism, or while singing a worship song whose chords tug at our heart strings, we can feel like maybe the experience was not as profound as it was supposed to be. As a result, many Christians have had to cope with a prowling anxiety about the realness or maturity of their faith. This is especially true for our brothers and sisters in Christ whose God-given temperaments are less expressive.

In a spiritual context where feelings are paramount, the ordinary is devalued. Actions are suspect. Habits are not to be trusted. Going through the motions seems almost sacrilegious. In his book *A Long Obedience in the Same Direction*, Eugene Peterson counters this myopic thinking: "We live in what one writer has called the 'age of sensation.' We think that if we don't feel something there can be no authenticity in doing it. But the wisdom of God says something different: that we can act ourselves into a new way of feeling much quicker than we can feel ourselves into a new way of acting. Worship is an act that develops feelings for God, not a feeling for God that is expressed in an act of worship."[1]

Most of us look for mountaintop emotional experiences in our lives of faith, where we feel a profound sense of the Holy Spirit's work in us, like a life-giving wind in our sails. We're not wrong to desire such transformative moments and to experience (and reexperience) the joy that comes with them. And sometimes we do have those experiences, and they can be life-defining forks in the road. But most of our spiritual lives unfold in more mundane ways, in rhythms that are daily, weekly, monthly, and more intermittent.

Jesus had a spiritual life too. It can strike us as an odd notion that Jesus had a spiritual life. It seems beneath him to speak of his *having* a spiritual life. Isn't it the case that he simply *is* spiritual life, the living source of all our spiritual lives? The answer, of course, is yes. But as we've seen, Jesus lived a real, human life too. He was a first-century Galilean Jew, with all the personal, social, political, emotional, and—yes—spiritual conventions that accompanied life in that historical context. Jesus had a spiritual life, and it mirrored the rhythms of his wider community, and to some extent the cadence of our modern spiritual lives. Let's explore the more routine aspects of his spiritual life and find what resonance we can with our own.

THE TEMPLE AND FESTIVALS

The Jerusalem temple was the epicenter of Jewish religious life during Jesus's years on earth. The Jews were spread out and woven into population centers around the Mediterranean world, but the temple in Jerusalem still beckoned them from afar to their spiritual hometown. It's hard to overstate the importance of the Jerusalem temple in Jewish life. This was where the sacrifices and offerings took place, where the priesthood was based, and where the chief priests and other spiritual authorities were headquartered. Local synagogues were multiplying throughout the Roman world, but they were no substitute for the Jerusalem temple, which had stood—in some form—for a millennium.[2]

Jesus and his family would have traveled regularly to Jerusalem for certain rituals and sacrifices as well as for national holidays. They would have known every landmark, every nook and cranny of the path from Nazareth to the temple. Shortly after Jesus's birth, Mary and Joseph went to Jerusalem to consecrate their child and make a specified offering: "When the time came for the purification rites required by the Law of Moses, Joseph and Mary took him to Jerusalem to present him to the Lord (as it is written in the Law of the Lord, 'Every firstborn male is to be consecrated to the Lord'), and to offer a sacrifice in keeping with what is said in the Law of the Lord: 'a pair of doves or two young pigeons' (Luke 2:22–24).

When we read about moments like this, we can feel like they're extraordinary because Jesus's birth was miraculous and because we don't perform such ritual sacrifices in our faith life today. But this practice of dedicating a child at the temple was as ordinary to Jesus's family as a twenty-first-century child dedication ceremony at church or even a toddler smashing a cupcake at their first birthday party. Many Jewish families did this and would have shared the happy news with their friends and relatives, remembering the moment for years to come.

There were several annual holidays and festivals that Jesus would have participated in over the course of his life, and these occasions involved trips to Jerusalem along with tens of thousands of other pilgrims from all over the Mediterranean world. These festivals are still celebrated in the modern state of Israel and in Jewish communities around the world. One such festival that Jesus attended was Passover, which occurs in the springtime. It is a remembrance of Israel's past when they were delivered from Egypt during the exodus. Jesus's arrest, trial, and crucifixion happened against the backdrop of the Passover, but this was hardly his first time celebrating the holiday in Jerusalem. The Gospels record that Jesus's family regularly celebrated Passover in Jerusalem: "Every year Jesus' parents went to Jerusalem for the Festival of the Passover. When he was twelve years old, they went up to the festival, according to the custom" (vv. 41–42). Jesus's Passover memories would have been about travel to Jerusalem, special offerings, family meals, crowded worship services in the temple courts, and retellings of the exodus.

Jesus also celebrated the Festival of Tabernacles in Jerusalem, which happens in the autumn. This festival is a celebratory remembrance of God's provision during Israel's years of wandering in the desert after gaining their freedom from Egypt. Again, travel from Galilee to Jerusalem would have been a big part of Jesus's experiences of Tabernacles, as well as the practice of living in a booth (or hut) for a week in order to intentionally recall the nomadic years of Israel's ancestors. There were worship services and other communal rituals at the temple, and the streets of Jerusalem would be packed with pilgrims from all over. The gospel of John records Jesus traveling to Jerusalem for this holiday, a trip he ordinarily would have taken with his family:

> When the Jewish Festival of Tabernacles was near, Jesus' brothers said to him, "Leave Galilee and go

> to Judea, so that your disciples there may see the works you do." . . .
>
> After his brothers had left for the festival, he went also, not publicly, but in secret. . . .
>
> Not until halfway through the festival did Jesus go up to the temple courts and begin to teach. (7:2–3, 10, 14)

When Jesus's unbelieving brothers goaded him about the Festival of Tabernacles, their memories would have undoubtedly returned to years gone by when they traveled with their eldest brother to Jerusalem for earlier festivals. Going to the Festival of Tabernacles was as familiar to Jesus's family as Thanksgiving dinner is to Americans. In fact, this was one of the most popular Jewish festivals of Jesus's day.[3]

We also know that Jesus celebrated the Festival of Dedication, or Hanukkah. This happened in the winter and was a remembrance of a time two centuries before Jesus's life when the Jews rose up against their Greek overlords, gained independence, and rededicated the Jerusalem temple to its intended purpose. This festival did not require Jews to travel to Jerusalem, so most years Jesus's family probably celebrated at their home or synagogue in Nazareth. They lit oil lamps and recalled God's faithfulness during a dark chapter of Israel's history. The gospel of John records Jesus's presence in Jerusalem for this festival: "Then came the Festival of Dedication at Jerusalem. It was winter, and Jesus was in the temple courts walking in Solomon's Colonnade. The Jews who were there gathered around him, saying, 'How long will you keep us in suspense? If you are the Messiah, tell us plainly'" (10:22–24).

The only thing unusual about Jesus's presence at these festivals was that he had begun his public ministry, and people knew who he was. He was teaching and taking on a public role, which was new, but he had celebrated these festivals—and others—dozens of times in his life without any fanfare. These festivals had a holiday feel to them.

We too can look back over our lives and remember a handful of unusually special Christmas or Easter celebrations. I recall spending Christmas with my mom's side of the family in New England a couple times when I was a kid. My family didn't live in a cold climate, so the memories of snow on the ground, heavy winter coats, sledding, and frost-covered cars will always stick with me. I remember hearing "Feliz Navidad" on the radio while we waited—somewhat impatiently—for our rental car's windows to defrost so that we could go open presents at my grandparents' house on Christmas morning.

There were other notable or unusual holiday celebrations over the years, but most of them were routine. They were still deeply meaningful and special, but in an ordinary way. These holidays are about spending time with family and friends and remembering what we're thankful for. The holidays put things into perspective, and they give us a sense of connection to the wider Christian community around the world that celebrates with us. Meaningful, but ordinary. We know how that feels. Jesus's experiences at the annual Jerusalem festivals must have felt comparable.

SYNAGOGUE

If the pilgrimage festivals in Jerusalem felt routine, then Jesus's weekly synagogue participation would have felt even more so. The synagogue was the hub of religious life, where regular worship services were held on the Sabbath and on other days, with prayer, singing, and the studying of Scripture. The synagogues also served more broadly as community centers. They hosted events, provided educational opportunities, and even served as lodging for travelers.[4] A first-century inscription was discovered in Jerusalem that outlines the various functions of the synagogue: "Theodotus, son of Vettenus, priest and archisynagogue, son of an archisynagogue, built the synagogue for the reading of the law and the teaching of the commandments, and the guest-house and the rooms and the water supplies as an inn for those who have need when they come from abroad; which synagogue his fathers founded and the elders and Simonides."[5]

Jesus must have been to hundreds of synagogue worship services in his lifetime, and his family would have visited their local synagogue for many other reasons over the years. Luke gives us a glance at how routine his synagogue participation was: "He went to Nazareth, where he had been brought up, and on the Sabbath day he went into the synagogue, as was his custom" (Luke 4:16). In the Gospels, synagogues are the locations for many of Jesus's most extraordinary actions, interactions, and teachings.[6] But the fact that he was in the synagogues was by no means out of the ordinary.

So, the weekly rhythm of Jesus's spiritual life was rather ordinary for about three decades of his life. This does not mean it wasn't meaningful. We in the modern church experience similar rhythms of church worship services, small groups, youth group events, Bible studies, and other regular opportunities to engage in the life of the church. These experiences often feel meaningful, but they are not extraordinary or necessarily very emotional. Jesus had experiences like this too.

PRAYER AND OTHER PERSONAL PRACTICES

The great Jerusalem festivals and local synagogue services were national and communal affairs. Jesus also had a personal spiritual life that was—again—routine and ordinary. It goes without saying that his relationship with his heavenly Father was singularly special, but the basics of his daily religious practices were similar to what most Jews of his day prioritized. Jesus engaged in personal prayer, as we've seen already, often seeking out solitude for these important experiences. He observed the weekly Sabbath, read the Scriptures, and followed the dietary restrictions of the Old Testament.

We have these ordinary personal spiritual practices too. We seek to understand the Scriptures. We strive to follow God's commands in the minutiae of daily decisions. We pray. These practices rarely feel extraordinary at the time, but their collective effect on our life is significant.

OUR EVERYDAY MOMENTS

We have considered three levels of routine spiritual experiences in Jesus's life: national festivals, community synagogue participation, and personal devotion. These practices reflected the widespread habits of first-century Jews, and in that sense they were routine. In the words of Shaye Cohen, most Jews of Jesus's day "observed the Sabbath and the holidays, heard the scriptural lessons in the synagogue on Sabbath, abstained from forbidden foods, purified themselves before entering the temple precincts, circumcised their sons on the eighth day, and adhered to the ethical norms of folk piety."[7]

Going through the motions gets a bad rap. I suppose if what we mean by "going through the motions" is that we don't care or our heart isn't in it, then the bad rap is justified. That is not what we're going for in our lives of faith. But if "going through the motions" means that our lives of faith unfold with some level of predictability and routine, which can over time provide sturdy scaffolding for spiritual growth, then we should thank God not only for the mountaintop experiences but also for the mundane ones: weekly worship, daily prayer, occasional fasting, the regular study of Scripture, and fellowship with other Christians. If the ordinary aspects of faith were a vital part of Jesus's spiritual life, then we certainly should guard against viewing the more routine elements of our faith lives as inconsequential. Their cumulative effect over the course of our lives should not be underestimated.

QUESTIONS FOR GROUP DISCUSSION OR PERSONAL REFLECTION

- What surprised or challenged you about this chapter?
- What is one mountaintop moment in your spiritual life that made a deep impression on you?
- What are the more ordinary elements of your faith that unfold with little fanfare?
- How do the ordinary, routine aspects of your faith interact with the emotional high points? How do you think they work together for your spiritual growth?
- In what ways might you need to grow in your understanding and practice of the routine parts of your spiritual life?
- If you could ask Jesus something about your spiritual life and get an audible answer right now, what would you ask and why?

Dear Jesus, help me not to look down on routine spiritual experiences as if they're unimportant or less formative than emotional ones. Help me to trust that you are using all of my life experiences—from the moving to the mundane—to form me into your likeness. Help me to see the seemingly repetitive elements of my spiritual life as a hammer in your hands, chiseling me each day into the shape you want me to grow into. As the psalmist says, let the routine elements of my spiritual life have a rooting function, as if I am a tree planted by flowing water, where I am nourished in a consistent way over the years of my life. Bring to my remembrance, Lord Jesus, that you too had a routine spiritual life. Encourage me through my prayers, the study of the Scriptures, and attendance of worship services. Help me to see other habits and disciplines that I can incorporate into my life. I trust you. Amen.

CONCLUSION

A Set Sun Still Shines

Do you trust in Jesus, in his humanity?

This was the question that began our journey and has resonated in the background of these past dozen or so chapters. In the poetic prologue to his gospel, John—Jesus's closest friend—wrote that the Son of God "became flesh and made his dwelling among us" (1:14). By now we have seen that this sojourn in human flesh was a true, three-dimensional, fully formed, authentically human experience for Jesus. He did not keep real human life at arm's length; he lived it as we do.

Jesus was human too.

But there's more to the story. We must speak of Jesus's humanity not only in the past tense (he *was* human) but also in the present tense.

Jesus is human still.

This may be hard for us to comprehend, because his post-resurrection humanness was supernatural, going beyond what we think of as possible for ordinary humans. Jesus appeared and disappeared. He moved through walls. At times people who knew him well did not recognize him. On the other hand, he was clearly in tangible, physical human form: people touched him, he conversed with his friends, he walked on the beach and ate food just like we do.

When Jesus ascended into heaven, he did not undergo a visible metamorphosis like he did during his earlier transfiguration on the mountaintop that Peter, James, and John witnessed. He left earth in his post-resurrection human form. He went to heaven as a human. Luke describes his departure:

> When he had led them out to the vicinity of Bethany, he lifted up his hands and blessed them. While he was blessing them, he left them and was taken up into heaven. (Luke 24:50–51)

> [Jesus] was taken up before their very eyes, and a cloud hid him from their sight.
>
> They were looking intently up into the sky as he was going, when suddenly two men dressed in white stood beside them. "Men of Galilee," they said, "why do you stand here looking into the sky? This same Jesus, who has been taken from you into heaven, will come back in the same way you have seen him go into heaven." (Acts 1:9–11)

Luke describes Jesus's disciples watching him closely, peering upward—astonished—as Jesus left earth, just as you or I would if someone we knew began to fly toward heaven. Jesus ascended into heaven and currently sits exalted at the highest place, but he has not lost his humanity in the process. Theologian Michael Bird summarizes Jesus's present humanity: "When Jesus was resurrected, he was still God incarnate, except now he had a glorified human body. When he ascended into heaven, he took that human body to heaven. He did not cease to be human. He did not shed his human shell like someone taking off a gorilla suit and resume his preincarnate life as a luminous and angelic being. No, he retains his glorified humanity for the rest of eternity."[1]

We cannot fully grasp the nature of Jesus's glorified, eternal body that is still somehow human. The good news is that we don't have to understand it to find comfort in his continued humanity. We don't have to feel like we personally relate to his present circumstances. We can simply trust that Jesus was human, he still is, and he knows exactly how to relate to us.

My grandpa was one of the most important people in my life, and I loved him so much. He was a pastor and a longtime US Army chaplain serving here and abroad. He retired as a lieutenant colonel. Grandpa's kindness, humor, plainspoken wisdom, and sunny outlook on life made a deep impression on me, and I turned to him for counsel on countless occasions, especially as I began to follow his footsteps into ministry.

In the summer of 2023, my family moved halfway across the country for me to begin a new pastoral position. As usual, I turned to my family—including my grandpa—for advice and prayers during the whole process of searching for a new position, accepting this one, and pulling up roots in one state and putting down new ones in another. Grandpa was thrilled about the new chapter in my family's life, and we spoke often about it.

During the week when we traveled from Texas to the Carolinas, my grandpa started to feel sick. Being in his mid-nineties, he was taken to the hospital as a precaution. I still have upbeat voicemails from him that he sent from his hospital bed, asking me how the trip was going and expressing his excitement about watching my new church's services online.

Grandpa went home from the hospital but did not improve. Just a few days after we arrived in our new home on the East Coast, he went to be with Jesus. A week earlier, no one expected his death was imminent. He had been an exceptionally healthy person his whole life. The day before he died, I got to speak to my grandpa briefly on the phone. I couldn't believe he was going to die soon. I told him I loved him, and I heard him say he loved me for what would be the last time in this life.

That evening, knowing he had hours—not days—left on this earth, I sat on the back porch of the lake house where my family was staying temporarily. I watched the sunset over Lake Wylie—one of the first sunsets in our new home. As the sun dipped toward the horizon, it became fiery orange. It further dimmed to the point that I could stare directly at the crimson star. Its reflection scattered across the lake like swirling globs of glowing paint, stirred up by the wake of boats passing by. I sat there and cried. As the sun disappeared below the trees, I thought about how Grandpa's life was disappearing too.

When the sun finally vanished behind the trees, I felt an alien sense of comfort, one that seemed to come from outside of me and that didn't make sense. The sun had disappeared. Its reflection on the water was no more. But there was still light. It wasn't total darkness. The sun didn't *actually* disappear. I just couldn't see it anymore. Its light remained—the magic hour, they call it—in that time between sunset and the darkness of night.

God used this experience to remind me that my grandpa still lives. He's just over the horizon. The light of his life still shines in a literal sense (Grandpa is alive with Jesus), and it still radiates into my family's life through the memories of his time with us. One day, those of us who know Jesus will all have our moment to sneak over the horizon and meet our Savior face-to-face, and someone else will have their magic hour thinking about us.

When Jesus ascended into heaven, he didn't actually disappear or cease to exist. He didn't stop living or being human. He's just stepped out of sight for a while, but his light still shines into our world and our lives through his Word, our faith, the church, and the ever-presence of the Holy Spirit.

As the sun sets on this book, let's close by returning briefly to Hebrews 4, the main scriptural lens for what we've explored together. Hebrews 4 closes with a trio of powerful verses describing what Jesus—our high priest—is like and what he means for our lives today.

In the first of the three verses, the author draws our attention to Jesus's ascension: "Therefore, since we have a great high priest who has ascended into heaven, Jesus the Son of God, let us hold firmly to the faith we profess" (v. 14). Jesus has given us all the reasons we need to trust in him: he came to earth out of his love for us, he willingly gave his life for us on the cross, he died but did not stay dead, and—having been reunited with his human body—he ascended into heaven. This was Jesus's experience, and it will one day be the experience of each of us who calls him Lord and Savior. Because of this, we can hold firmly to the faith we profess.

The second verse we have already seen at the beginning of this book and in the interlude as our primary scriptural impetus for studying Jesus's human life: "For we do not have a high priest who is unable to empathize with our weaknesses, but we have one who has been tempted in every way, just as we are—yet he did not sin" (v. 15). Jesus is not unable to empathize with our weaknesses. He can and does empathize. As a human, he was tested in every way, just as we are. Together we have examined numerous facets of his testing. He had a home life that felt mixed-up. His work life was not always easy. He was well acquainted with human frailty, illness, and death. He was criticized by many people, even his family, after he became a public figure. He struggled to find private time for himself. His financial life was mentally and physically taxing. He felt big feelings and walked through heavy emotional territory. He lived in a culturally fractured context. He had to swat away political frustrations on a regular basis and navigated the fuzzy lines between his various social circles. While he had a special relationship with his heavenly Father, he also had a routine spiritual life that unfolded in a regular cadence. He knew how it felt to be lonely and to be full of joy. His human life was not merely biological; it was experiential. He understands what it's like to be us.

But how does that affect our lives?

The final verse of Hebrews 4 gives us the answer. What is the purpose of having a greater understanding of the historical backdrop and personal experiences of Jesus's life? What do we do with all this information? Hebrews 4:16 gives us our action step: "Let us then approach God's throne of grace with confidence, so that we may receive mercy and find grace to help us in our time of need."

When we are in times of need, struggle, disorientation, disillusionment, or despair, we should turn to God. Many of us know that, but the *way* we turn to God matters. Are we turning to him sheepishly? Are we afraid he won't understand or accept us? Do we feel we are bothering him or wasting his time? Are we worried that disapproving judgment is his main feeling about us? Are we concerned that he won't forgive us when we make sinful choices? Hebrews 4 tells us that because Jesus has been tested in every way as we are, we can approach his throne of grace with *confidence*. That's how we should turn to God in times of trouble: confidently. He stands ready to offer mercy, grace, forgiveness, wisdom, and help, given from an infinitely deep well of love and a wealth of his own human experiences.

We often wonder why God allows us to suffer and struggle in life. When we ponder those important questions, we should always remind ourselves that he allowed himself to suffer and struggle too. He could have forever watched us face trouble from a safe distance, but he didn't.

Jesus knows what our lives are like because of his own experiences, but he also knows us as individuals more than we could ever possibly imagine. As the psalmist says,

> You have searched me, Lord,
>   and you know me.
> You know when I sit and when I rise;
>   you perceive my thoughts from afar.
> You discern my going out and my lying down;
>   you are familiar with all my ways.
> Before a word is on my tongue
>   you, Lord, know it completely.
>
> (Psalm 139:1–4)

Or as Jesus said when teaching about prayer: "When you pray, do not keep on babbling like pagans, for they think they will be heard because of their many words. Do not be like them, for your Father knows what you need before you ask him" (Matthew 6:7–8).

When Peter, one of Jesus's closest friends, addressed his brothers and sisters in Christ about the recent influx of Gentiles into the church—which was making some Jewish Christians uncomfortable—he said this: "Brothers, you know that some time ago God made a choice among you that the Gentiles might hear from my lips the message of the gospel and believe. God, who knows the heart, showed that he accepted them by giving the Holy Spirit to them, just as he did to us" (Acts 15:7–8).

The key phrase is "God, who knows the heart." What Peter literally said, in the ancient Greek, is that God is the "heart knower" (*kardiognōstēs*). Jesus's best friend, John, picked up this same idea in one of his letters: "If our hearts condemn us, we know that God is greater than our hearts, and he knows everything" (1 John 3:20).

God is the knower of hearts. He knows us perfectly, not only because of his divine omniscience but because of Jesus's human experiences.

You are human.

Jesus was human too.

Jesus is human still.

You have a heart, and Jesus had one too. He still does. Open your heart—your soul, your life—to him, confident that you arc truly known, fully understood, and perfectly loved. Offer yourself to him, holding nothing back, and you'll be glad you did.

QUESTIONS FOR GROUP DISCUSSION OR PERSONAL REFLECTION

- What surprised or challenged you about this book?
- How has your faith in Jesus deepened or been shaped by what you've discovered in these pages?
- What obstacles stand in the way of you turning to Jesus with confidence in your times of trouble?
- What do you want to learn next about God? How can you take steps to pursue those answers?
- If you could ask Jesus something about his time on earth and get an audible answer right now, what would you ask and why?

Dear Jesus, thank you for giving me so many gifts in my life. Eyes to see. Parents and teachers who helped me learn to read. The ability to read your Word so I can grow in my knowledge of and relationship with you. I want to find confidence,

Lord, in how well you know me. As the writer of Hebrews explained, you were tested in all the ways that I am, and because of that, I can turn to you confidently, knowing you truly understand my experiences. I want to turn to you in that way, but I confess I sometimes worry that you don't understand or wonder whether you care. I especially wonder if you care when I've made mistakes or chosen to sin in some way. I confess that this is a failure of faith on my part, and a lack of imagination. Enlarge my imagination, Lord, to see you as someone who really sees me. When times of trouble come my way, which is more often than I want, let it be my instinctive response to turn to you for help. Give me opportunities to encourage others to turn to you in the same way. You are the knower of hearts, and I'm thankful that you made mine and know me so well. Amen.

Notes

Introduction: More Than Biology

1. To use the title of Josh McDowell's classic book *More Than a Carpenter*.
2. Max Zerwick and Mary Grosvenor, *A Grammatical Analysis of the Greek New Testament* (Gregorian and Biblical Press, 2013), 662; Frederick W. Danker et al., *A Greek-English Lexicon of the New Testament and Other Early Christian Literature* (University of Chicago Press, 2000), 792–93.
3. Because we're focused on Jesus's time on earth, I've so far referred to Jesus's humanity in the past tense: *Jesus Was Human Too*. However, Jesus did not leave his human body behind when he ascended into heaven. The present tense nature of his humanity will be addressed in the conclusion of the book.

Chapter 1: A Mixed-Up Home Life

1. Max Zerwick and Mary Grosvenor, *A Grammatical Analysis of the Greek New Testament* (Gregorian and Biblical Press, 2013), 1; Frederick W. Danker et al., *A Greek-English Lexicon of the New Testament and Other Early Christian Literature* (University of Chicago Press, 2000), 656.

2. Lynn Cohick, *Women in the World of the Earliest Christians* (Baker Academic, 2009), 153. Everett Ferguson describes the nature of the ancient marriage contract: "The marriage was a contract between families. It was effected in two stages: the betrothal (or 'acquisition' of the bride), and the wedding proper (taking the bride into the husband's home). The betrothal had the legal force of marriage and could be broken only by divorce (Matt. 1:18–19). It was accomplished by the bridegroom paying the bride-price (or a part of it) or delivering a deed. The customary written contract included the husband's duties to his wife and the sum due her in the event of a divorce or his death." Ferguson, *Backgrounds of Early Christianity*, 3rd ed. (Eerdmans, 2003), 74.
3. Cohick, *Women in the World of the Earliest Christians*, 153.
4. Stephen C. Carlson, "The Accommodations of Joseph and Mary in Bethlehem: Κατάλυμα in Luke 2.7," *New Testament Studies* 56, no. 3 (2010): 336. See also Howard Marshall, *The Gospel of Luke*, New International Greek Testament Commentary (Eerdmans, 1978), 101.
5. For instance, Francisco Sánchez de las Brozas in the sixteenth century, and Stephen Carlson in the twenty-first century.
6. Carlson, "The Accommodations of Joseph and Mary in Bethlehem," 333. Carlson's grammatical and historical analysis underpins much of what I say here about the circumstances in Bethlehem.
7. Ferguson, *Backgrounds of Early Christianity*, 74; Carlson, "The Accommodations of Joseph and Mary in Bethlehem," 339.
8. Luke's language in 2:6 is literally, "In the being there [i.e., in Bethlehem], the days were fulfilled for her to give birth." The mention of "days" in the original Greek implies a longer stay in Bethlehem than the sense of immediacy conveyed by the English translation.

9. Carlson, "The Accommodations of Joseph and Mary in Bethlehem," 334–35.
10. Carlson, "The Accommodations of Joseph and Mary in Bethlehem," 341–42.
11. Jesus was born not in the year 0 but probably a handful of years earlier—around 6–4 BC. We know this because King Herod tried to have the infant Jesus killed, and historians are quite certain Herod died in the spring of 4 BC. Our calendars are off by a few years because the monk who conceived the BC–AD division several centuries later made some errors when calculating the date of Jesus's birth. See Colin Nicholl, *The Great Christ Comet: Revealing the True Star of Bethlehem* (Crossway, 2015), 42.
12. F. F. Bruce, *New Testament History* (Doubleday, 1969), 135–36.
13. Bruce, *New Testament History*, 135–36. See also Michael Grant, *The Jews in the Roman World* (Dorset Press, 1984), 59.
14. Robert H. Mounce, "Nazareth," in *International Standard Bible Encyclopedia*, vol. 3, ed. Geoffrey W. Bromiley et al. (Eerdmans, 1986), 500–501.
15. Rainer Riesner, "Archaeology and Geography," in *Dictionary of Jesus and the Gospels* (InterVarsity Press, 1992), 36.
16. Thomas O. Lambdin, *Introduction to Sahidic Coptic* (Mercer University Press, 1983), vii.
17. Years later after Jesus's resurrection, his brothers James and Jude became leaders in the early church, authoring the New Testament books bearing their names.

Chapter 2: A Strenuous Work Life

1. Craig Blomberg, *Matthew*, New American Commentary 22 (B&H Publishing, 1992), 228.
2. Grant Osborne, *Matthew*, Exegetical Commentary on the New Testament (Zondervan, 2010), 550.

3. Max Zerwick and Mary Grosvenor, *A Grammatical Analysis of the Greek New Testament* (Gregorian and Biblical Press, 2013), 45; Frederick W. Danker et al., *A Greek-English Lexicon of the New Testament and Other Early Christian Literature* (University of Chicago Press, 2000), 995. The word *tectonic* comes from the same ancient Greek word. Plate tectonics got its name because it has to do with the "structure of the earth's crust"; Online Etymological Dictionary, "tectonic," last modified September, 10, 2022, https://www.etymonline.com/word/tectonic#etymonline_v_7667.
4. Osborne, *Matthew*, 550; "Roman Crucifixion Methods Reveal the History of Crucifixion," Biblical Archaeological Society, August 17, 2024, https://www.biblicalarchaeology.org/daily/biblical-topics/crucifixion/roman-crucifixion-methods-reveal-the-history-of-crucifixion/.
5. James F. Strange, "Galilee," in *Dictionary of New Testament Background*, ed. Craig A. Evans and Stanley E. Porter (InterVarsity Press, 2000), 395.
6. *The Surprises of Sepphoris*, *Frontline*, PBS, April 1998, https://www.pbs.org/wgbh/pages/frontline/shows/religion/jesus/sepphoris.html; Mark Chancey, "How Jewish Was Jesus's Galilee?," in *The Galilee Jesus Knew* (Biblical Archaeological Society, 2008), 4.
7. Josephus, *Antiquities of the Jews*, 18.2; F. F. Bruce, *New Testament History* (Doubleday, 1969), 27–28.
8. *The Surprises of Sepphoris*; Craig Blomberg, *Jesus and the Gospels*, 2nd ed. (B&H Academic, 2009), 430; Strange, "Galilee," 396–97; Chancey, "How Jewish Was Jesus's Galilee?," 2–5.
9. Chancey, "How Jewish Was Jesus's Galilee?," 2, 5.

Chapter 3: A Precarious Physical Life

1. The Greek word is *hēlikia*; see also Luke 19:3; John 9:21; Frederick W. Danker et al., *A Greek-English Lexicon of*

the New Testament and Other Early Christian Literature (University of Chicago Press, 2000), 435–36.

2. Lynn H. Cohick, *Women in the World of the Earliest Christians* (Baker Academic, 2009), 135.
3. John T. Fitzgerald, "Orphans in Mediterranean Antiquity and Early Christianity," *Acta Theologica* 36, suppl. 23 (2016): 31.
4. Susan Weingarten, "Biblical Archaeology 101: The Ancient Diet of Roman Palestine," *Biblical Archaeology Review* 45, no. 2 (2019): https://library.biblicalarchaeology.org/article/biblical-archaeology-101-the-ancient-diet-of-roman-palestine/.
5. Fitzgerald, "Orphans in Mediterranean Antiquity and Early Christianity," 30–31.
6. R. K. Harrison, "Disease," in *International Standard Bible Encyclopedia*, vol. 1, ed. Geoffrey W. Bromiley et al. (Eerdmans, 1979), 958–59.

Chapter 4: A Criticized Public Life

1. F. F. Bruce, *New Testament History* (Doubleday, 1969), 96–100; Terence L. Donaldson, "Zealot," in *International Standard Bible Encyclopedia*, vol. 4, ed. Geoffrey W. Bromiley et al. (Eerdmans, 1988), 1179; W. J. Heard and C. A. Evans, "Jewish Revolutionary Movements," in *Dictionary of New Testament Background*, ed. Craig A. Evans and Stanley E. Porter (InterVarsity Press, 2000), 945–56; Everett Ferguson, *Backgrounds of Early Christianity*, 3rd ed. (Eerdmans, 2003), 532.
2. Matthew 10:4; Mark 3:18; Luke 6:15; Acts 1:13.
3. Ferguson, *Backgrounds of Early Christianity*, 532; Thom R. Schreiner, "Simon (NT)," in *International Standard Bible Encyclopedia*, 4:515.

Chapter 5: An Elusive Private Life

1. Frederick W. Danker et al., *A Greek-English Lexicon of the New Testament and Other Early Christian Literature* (University of Chicago Press, 2000), 391–92.
2. Henry David Thoreau, *Walden, or Life in the Woods* (Ticknor and Fields, 1854), 5.
3. Henri Nouwen, *Out of Solitude: Three Meditations on the Christian Life* (Ave Maria Press, 2008), 25–26.

Chapter 6: An Insecure Financial Life

1. According to the American Psychological Association's 2015 Stress in America survey, "72 percent of Americans reported feeling stressed about money at least some time in the prior month" (Linda Gallo, "Speaking of Psychology: The Stress of Money," American Psychological Association, 2015, https://www.apa.org/news/podcasts/speaking-of-psychology/financial-stress). The 2022 edition of the Stress in America survey showed continuing levels of financial stress, especially related to inflation. In 2023, according to Capital One's CreditWise Survey, 73 percent of Americans view their finances as their most significant source of stress (Alexandria White, "73% of Americans Rank Their Finances as the No. 1 Stress in Life, according to New Capitol One CreditWise Survey," CNBC, last modified May 20, 2024, https://www.cnbc.com/select/73-percent-of-americans-rank-finances-as-the-number-one-stress-in-life/).
2. Daniel Kahneman and Angus Deaton, "High Income Improves Evaluation of Life but Not Emotional Well-Being," *Psychological and Cognitive Sciences* 107, no. 38 (September 7, 2010): 16489–93; Adela Suliman, "Can Money Buy Happiness? Scientists Say It Can," *Washington Post*, March 8, 2023, https://www.washingtonpost.com/business/2023/03/08/money-wealth-happiness-study/.

3. Grant Edward Donnelly, Tianyi Zheng, Emily Haisley, and Michael I. Norton, "The Amount and Source of Millionaires' Wealth (Moderately) Predict Their Happiness," *Personality and Social Psychology Bulletin* 44, no. 5 (May 2018): 684–99; cf. Joe Pinsker, "The Reason Many Ultrarich People Aren't Satisfied with Their Wealth," *Atlantic* (December 4, 2018), https://www.theatlantic.com/family/archive/2018/12/rich-people-happy-money/577231/.
4. Matthew 9:9; 17:24–27; Luke 19:1–9; 20:20–26; 23:1–3.
5. Everett Ferguson, *Backgrounds of Early Christianity*, 3rd ed. (Eerdmans, 2003), 95–96; D. W. J. Gill, "Greco-Roman Taxation," in *Dictionary of New Testament Background*, ed. Craig A. Evans and Stanley E. Porter (InterVarsity Press, 2000), 1161–63; Thomas E. Schmidt, "Jewish Taxation," in *Dictionary of New Testament Background*, 1163–66; A. N. Sherwin-White, *Roman Society and Roman Law in the New Testament* (Clarendon Press, 1963), 125–26.

Chapter 7: A Heavy Emotional Life

1. Max Zerwick and Mary Grosvenor, *A Grammatical Analysis of the Greek New Testament* (Gregorian and Biblical Press, 2013), 321.
2. Frederick W. Danker et al., *A Greek-English Lexicon of the New Testament and Other Early Christian Literature* (University of Chicago Press, 2000), 322.
3. Zerwick and Grosvenor, *A Grammatical Analysis of the Greek New Testament*, 321; Danker et al., *A Greek-English Lexicon of the New Testament*, 990–91.
4. Matthew 21:12–17; Mark 11:15–18; Luke 19:45–48; John 2:13–22.
5. Barclay M. Newman, *The UBS Greek New Testament: Reader's Edition with Textual Notes* (Deutsche Bibelgesellschaft, 2007), 704.

6. Zerwick and Grosvenor, *A Grammatical Analysis of the Greek New Testament*, 273.
7. C. S. Lewis, *Letters to Malcolm: Chiefly on Prayer* (HarperCollins, 1992), 56.

Chapter 8: A Fractured Cultural Life

1. For example, Caesarea Maritima, the Herodium, Masada, Tiberius, Sepphoris, and various projects within Jerusalem such as the temple and adjoining Antonia Fortress.
2. Larry Hurtado, *Destroyer of the Gods: Early Christian Distinctiveness in the Roman World* (Baylor University Press, 2016), 52–53.
3. H. G. M. Williamson and C. A. Evans, "Samaritans," in *Dictionary of New Testament Background*, ed. Craig A. Evans and Stanley E. Porter (InterVarsity Press, 2000), 1057.
4. Williamson and Evans, "Samaritans," 1059.
5. Josephus, *Antiquities of the Jews* 20.6.1, trans. William Whiston (Hendrickson, 1987), 532.
6. L. Michael White, "Galilee," *Frontline*, accessed February 11, 2025, https://www.pbs.org/wgbh/pages/frontline/shows/religion/portrait/galilee.html.
7. *'Erub.*, 53a–53b.
8. R. T. France, *The Gospel of Matthew* (Eerdmans, 2007), 6.

Chapter 9: A Troubling Political Life

1. F. F. Bruce, *New Testament History* (Doubleday, 1969), 32.
2. Bruce, *New Testament History*, 19.
3. Bruce, *New Testament History*, 34–37.
4. Josephus, *Antiquities of the Jews* 18.3.2; *Wars of the Jews* 2.9.4.
5. Bruce, *New Testament History*, 19.
6. Bruce, *New Testament History*, 33–34.
7. Bruce, *New Testament History*, 63–64.

8. H. W. Hoehner, "Herodian Dynasty," in *Dictionary of New Testament Background*, ed. Craig A. Evans and Stanley E. Porter (InterVarsity Press, 2000), 491.
9. Philo, Leg. Gai. (299–304); H. W. Hoehner, "Herodian Dynasty," 492.

Chapter 11: A Routine Spiritual Life

1. Eugene Peterson, *A Long Obedience in the Same Direction* (InterVarsity Press, 2019), 48.
2. F. F. Bruce, *New Testament History* (Doubleday, 1969), 138.
3. Everett Ferguson, *Backgrounds of Early Christianity*, 3rd ed. (Eerdmans, 2003), 559.
4. Ferguson, *Backgrounds of Early Christianity*, 575.
5. Corpus Inscriptionum Judaicarum 1404, in Ferguson, *Backgrounds of Early Christianity*, 575.
6. Debates, like the ones Jesus had with those questioning his authority, were commonplace in synagogues. See John 6:25–59; Jordan J. Ryan, "Jesus in the Synagogue," Biblical Archaeological Society, March 1, 2023, https://www.biblicalarchaeology.org/magazine/jesus-in-the-synagogue/.
7. Shaye Cohen, *From the Maccabees to the Mishnah*, 3rd ed. (Westminster John Knox Press, 2014), 171.

Conclusion: A Set Sun Still Shines

1. Michael Bird, *Evangelical Theology: A Biblical and Systematic Introduction*, 2nd ed. (Zondervan, 2020), 511.

Spread the Word by Doing One Thing.

- Give a copy of this book as a gift.
- Share the QR code link via your social media.
- Write a review of this book on your blog, favorite bookseller's website, or at ourdailybreadpublishing.org.
- Recommend this book to your church, small group, or book club.

Connect with us.

Our Daily Bread Publishing
PO Box 3566, Grand Rapids, MI 49501, USA
Email: books@odbm.org